TRAVERSE THEATRE

SCOTLAND'S NEW WRITING THEATRE

Traverse Theatre Company

Dark Earth

by David Harrower

Cast in order of appearance

Valerie	Frances Grey
Euan	John Mackay
Petey	Jimmy Yuill
Ida	Anne Lacey
Christine	Suzanne Donaldson

Director	Philip Howard
Designer	Fiona Watt
Lighting Designer	Neil Austin
Composer	John Irvine
Assistant Director	Lorne Campbell
Voice Coach	Ros Steen
Stage Manager	Lee Davies
Deputy Stage Manager	Gemma Smith
Assistant Stage Manager	Steven Muckersie

**First performed at the Traverse Theatre
Friday 25 July 2003**

TRAVERSE THEATRE

powerhouse of new writing DAILY TELEGRAPH

Artistic Director Philip Howard

The Traverse is Scotland's new writing theatre. Founded in 1963 by a group of maverick artists and enthusiasts, it began as an imaginative attempt to capture the spirit of adventure and experimentation of the Edinburgh Festival all year round. Throughout the decades, the Traverse has evolved and grown in artistic output and ambition. It has refined its mission by strengthening its commitment to producing new plays by Scottish and international playwrights and actively nurturing them throughout their careers. Traverse productions have been seen worldwide and tour regularly throughout the UK and overseas.

The Traverse has produced over 600 new plays in its lifetime and, through a spirit of innovation and risk-taking, has launched the careers of many of the country's best known writers. From, among others, Stanley Eveling in the 1960s, John Byrne in the 1970s, Liz Lochhead in the 1980s, to David Greig and David Harrower in the 1990s, the Traverse is unique in Scotland in its dedication to new writing. It fulfils the crucial role of providing the infrastructure, professional support and expertise to ensure the development of a dynamic theatre culture for Scotland.

The Traverse's activities encompass every aspect of playwriting and production, providing and facilitating play reading panels, script development workshops, rehearsed readings, public playwriting workshops, writers' groups, a public playwrights' platform, The Monday Lizard, discussions and special events. The Traverse's work with young people is of supreme importance and takes the form of encouraging playwriting through its flagship education project, Class Act, as well as the Traverse Young Writers Group.

Edinburgh's Traverse Theatre is a mini-festival in itself THE TIMES

From its conception in the 1960s, the Traverse has remained a pivotal venue during the Edinburgh Festival. It receives enormous critical and audience acclaim for its programming, as well as regularly winning awards. In 2001 the Traverse was awarded two Scotsman Fringe Firsts and two Herald Angels for its own productions of *Gagarin Way* and *Wiping My Mother's Arse* and a Herald Archangel for overall artistic excellence. In 2002 the Traverse again had the pick of the Fringe Festival productions with *Outlying Islands* and *Iron* winning awards and transferring to the Royal Court Theatre, London. During the year the Traverse also reinforced its international profile and touring activities with a European tour of *Gagarin Way* and a successful Highlands & Islands tour of *Homers*.

For further information on the Traverse Theatre's activities and history, an online resource is available at www.virtualtraverse.co.uk To find out about ways to support the Traverse, please contact Norman MacLeod, Development Manager, on 0131 228 3223.

WRITER

David Harrower   Previous work for the Traverse: KNIVES IN HENS
(also The Bush Theatre, London, 1995); KILL THE OLD TORTURE THEIR
YOUNG (1998). Other theatre: THE CHRYSALIDS (NT Connections,
1996); PRESENCE (Royal Court, 2001). Adaptations include SIX
CHARACTERS IN SEARCH OF AN AUTHOR (Young Vic, 2001);
WOYZECK (Edinburgh Lyceum, 2001); IVANOV (National Theatre,
2002); THE GIRL ON THE SOFA (EIF/Schaubühne, Berlin, 2002); PURPLE
(Shell/Connections project, 2003). A new version of Horvath's TALES
FROM THE VIENNA WOODS opens at the National in autumn 2003.

COMPANY BIOGRAPHIES

Neil Austin (Lighting Designer): For the Traverse: MR PLACEBO (co-production with Drum Theatre, Plymouth). Other theatre includes: A PRAYER FOR OWEN MEANY, THE WALLS, FURTHER THAN THE FURTHEST THING (National Theatre); CALIGULA (Donmar Warehouse); JAPES (Theatre Royal, Haymarket); FLESH WOUND, TRUST (Royal Court); CUCKOOS (BITE-Pit, Barbican); MONKEY (Young Vic); AMERICAN BUFFALO (Royal Exchange, Manchester); WORLD MUSIC, THE MODERNISTS (Sheffield Crucible); THE LADY IN THE VAN, PRETENDING TO BE ME (West Yorkshire Playhouse); GREAT EXPECTATIONS (Bristol Old Vic); KING HEDLEY II (Birmingham Rep and Tricycle); ROMEO AND JULIET, TWELFTH NIGHT (Liverpool Playhouse); LOVES WORK, CUCKOOS, VENECIA (Gate Theatre); CLOSER (Teatro Broadway, Buenos Aires). Musicals include: BABES IN ARMS (Cardiff International Festival of Musical Theatre); SPEND, SPEND, SPEND (UK Tour – co-design with Mark Henderson); MY FAIR LADY (Teatro Nacional, Buenos Aires); BONNIE AND CLYDE (Guildhall). Operas include: THE EMBALMER (Almeida Opera); ORFEO (Opera City, Tokyo); PULSE SHADOWS (Queen Elizabeth Hall); L'ENFANT PRODIGUE, LE PORTRAIT DE MANON (Guildhall).

Lorne Campbell (Assistant Director): Lorne's assistant directorship at the Traverse is funded by Channel 4 Theatre Director Scheme. For the Traverse: MR PLACEBO, HOMERS, CLASS ACT. Before joining the Traverse he ran Forge Theatre Company for four years. His directing credits include: DEATH AND THE MAIDEN; THE CHEVIOT, THE STAG AND THE BLACK BLACK OIL; THE CHAIRS; THE DUMB WAITER; COMEDY OF ERRORS; OLEANNA. Trained: MA at RSAMD, BA at Liverpool John Moores.

Suzanne Donaldson (*Christine*): Suzanne has just graduated from Queen Margaret University College. Her college productions include: THE BALD PRIMA DONNA, A MIDSUMMER NIGHTS DREAM, GUID SISTERS, VICTORIA, THE SUICIDE. Also: A SOLEMN MASS FOR A FULL MOON IN SUMMER (Fringe 2002).

Frances Grey (*Valerie*): Theatre includes PLAYHOUSE CREATURES (West Yorkshire Playhouse); PLATONOV (Almeida); REBECCA (Royal Lyceum). Television includes: THE KEY, MESSIAH, MESSIAH 2: VENGEANCE IS MINE, MURDER IN MIND, VANITY FAIR, ACCUSED (BBC); THE SECRET WORLD OF MICHAEL FRY (Channel 4); REACH FOR THE MOON (LWT); TAGGART (Scottish Television). Film includes: JANICE BEARD 45wpm (Sweet Child Films).

Philip Howard (Director): Philip trained at the Royal Court Theatre, London, on the Regional Theatre Young Director Scheme from 1988-90. He was Associate Director at the Traverse from 1993-96, and has been Artistic Director since 1996. Productions for the Traverse include: HOMERS,

OUTLYING ISLANDS, THE BALLAD OF CRAZY PAOLA, WIPING MY MOTHER'S ARSE, THE TRESTLE AT POPE LICK CREEK, SHETLAND SAGA, SOLEMN MASS FOR A FULL MOON IN SUMMER (with Ros Steen), HIGHLAND SHORTS, THE SPECULATOR, HERITAGE (1998 and 2001), KILL THE OLD TORTURE THEIR YOUNG, THE CHIC NERDS, LAZYBED, WORMWOOD, FAITH HEALER, THE ARCHITECT, KNIVES IN HENS (also The Bush Theatre), EUROPE, BROTHERS OF THUNDER, LOOSE ENDS. Philip's other theatre includes: HIPPOLYTUS (Arts Theatre, Cambridge); ENTERTAINING MR SLOANE (Royal, Northampton); SOMETHING ABOUT US (Lyric Hammersmith Studio).

John Irvine (Composer): DARK EARTH is John's twentieth show for the Traverse. Other theatre work includes: KtC, Tron Theatre, Dundee Rep, Royal Lyceum (Edinburgh), Citizens Theatre, TAG, Gate Theatre (London) and Lung Ha's. John gained his PhD in music composition in 1999 from the University of Edinburgh and currently teaches at The City of Edinburgh Music School and St Mary's Music School.

Anne Lacey (*Ida*): Trained in Edinburgh, France and Italy. For the Traverse: SHETLAND SAGA, BONDAGERS, THE STRAW CHAIR, THE SILVER SPRIG. For Communicado: MARY QUEEN OF SCOTS GOT HER HEAD CHOPPED OFF, THE HOUSE WITH THE GREEN SHUTTERS, JOCK TAMSONS BAIRNS, THE CONE GATHERERS, TALL TALES. Anne has worked with many other companies including the Citizens', Old Vic, Dundee Rep, Raindog, Tron, lookOUT and the RSC. Television includes: three series as Esme in HAMISH MACBETH, DEACON BRODIE, DOCTOR FINLAY, KNOWING THE SCORE, RAB C. NESBITT, SWEET NOTHINGS, SHOOT FOR THE SUN, WILDFLOWERS, HOLBY CITY, MONARCH OF THE GLEN, TINSEL TOWN, STACEY STONE. Film includes: MY LIFE SO FAR, THIS YEARS LOVE, STRICTLY SINATRA. Shorts include: MIRROR, MIRROR, NAN, FISHY, PLAIN HUNGER. Radio short stories, play and comedy with BBC Radio.

John Mackay (*Evan*): Trained at Bristol Old Vic Theatre School. Theatre includes: AS YOU LIKE IT (Jaques); TROILUS AND CRESSIDA (Ulysses); THE WINTER'S TALE (Leontes); TWELFTH NIGHT (Aquecheek); MEASURE FOR MEASURE (Angelo); all for Shakespeare at the Tobacco Factory. Other theatre includes: ALL MY SONS (York Theatre Royal); WAR MUSIC (Sound & Fury); THAT'S ALL FOLKS, IDÉE FIXE (Bristol Old Vic). Television includes: CASUALTY (BBC); TRIAL AND RETRIBUTION III (ITV); DOC MARTIN (Buffalo Pictures). Radio includes: EVELINA, THE ILIAD, MADELEINE, HEART OF DARKNESS, NIGHT AND DAY, POETRY PLEASE, SOLDIER SOLDIER (BBC R4).

Ros Steen (Voice/Dialect Coach): Trained at RSAMD. Has worked extensively in theatre, film and TV. For the Traverse: HOMERS, OUTLYING ISLANDS, THE BALLAD OF CRAZY PAOLA, THE TRESTLE AT POPE LICK

CREEK, HERITAGE (2001 and 1998), AMONG UNBROKEN HEARTS, SHETLAND SAGA, SOLEMN MASS FOR A FULL MOON IN SUMMER (as co-director), KING OF THE FIELDS, HIGHLAND SHORTS, FAMILY, KILL THE OLD TORTURE THEIR YOUNG, THE CHIC NERDS, GRETA, LAZYBED, KNIVES IN HENS, PASSING PLACES, BONDAGERS, ROAD TO NIRVANA, SHARP SHORTS, MARISOL, GRACE IN AMERICA. Recent theatre work includes: DANCING AT LUGHNASA, DUCHESS OF MALFI, (Dundee Rep); BASH, DAMN JACOBITE BITCHES, OBSERVE THE SONS OF ULSTER MARCHING TOWARDS THE SOMME (Citizens' Theatre); WORD FOR WORD (Magnetic North); CAVE DWELLERS (7:84); EXILES (Jervis Young Directors/Young Vic); THE PRIME OF MISS JEAN BRODIE, PLAYBOY OF THE WESTERN WORLD (Royal Lyceum); SUNSET SONG (Prime Productions); THE BEAUTY QUEEN OF LEENANE (Tron); SINGLES NIGHT, HOME (lookOUT); THE PRICE (Brunton); TRAINSPOTTING (G & J Productions). Films include: SMALL LOVE, GREGORY'S TWO GIRLS. TV includes: ROCKFACE, 2000 ACRES OF SKY.

Fiona Watt (Designer): Fiona trained at Motley and was awarded an Arts Council of England Design Bursary in 1996. For the Traverse: OUTLYING ISLANDS, THE TRESTLE AT POPE LICK CREEK, HERITAGE, HIGHLANDS SHORTS. Other credits include: DEALER'S CHOICE (Tron); BOSTON MARRIAGE (Bolton Octagon); OUTWARD BOUND (Palace Theatre, Watford). Opera includes: ORPHEUS IN THE UNDERWORLD (British Youth Opera); LA TRAVIATA (Haddo House Opera); MAVRA, RIDERS TO THE SEA, GIANNI SCHICCHI, LA PIETRA DEL PARAGONE (RSAMD, Glasgow). Fiona has also worked extensively in theatre for young people, designing for TAG, Yorkshire Women and the Education Departments at Nottingham Playhouse, Theatre Clwyd and the Tricycle Theatre, London.

Jimmy Yuill (*Petey*): Started out at the Traverse in 1976 playing Will in THE JESUIT. Productions at Sheffield Crucible, Shared experience, Bush, Royal Court. For RSC: Snug in A MIDSUMMER NIGHTS DREAM, Laces in GOLDEN GIRLS, Wilfred Fox in TODAY, Young Wackford Squeers in NICHOLAS NICKELBY. For Renaissance Theatre Company: Friar Francis in MUCH ADO ABOUT NOTHING, Guildernstern in HAMLET, Corin in AS YOU LIKE IT, Kent in KING LEAR, Sicinius in CORIOLANUS, Teleysin in UNCLE VANYA. Most recent productions: Hastings in RICHARD III (Sheffield Crucible); Henry IV in HENRY IV Parts 1 & 2 (Bristol Old Vic). Television includes: THE INTERROGATION OF JOHN, BAD COMPANY, A MUG'S GAME, HAMISH MACBETH, DEMOB, TOUCH OF FROST, GRUSHKO, PSYCHOS, MONSIGNOR REYNARD, WYCLIFFE. Films include: LOCAL HERO, HENRY V, MUCH ADO ABOUT NOTHING, MARY SHELLEY'S FRANKENSTEIN, PAPER MASK, STRICTLY SINATRA, LOVES LABOURS LOST.

SPONSORSHIP

Sponsorship income enables the Traverse to commission
and produce new plays and to offer audiences a diverse and
exciting programme of events throughout the year

We would like to thank the following companies
for their support throughout the year

CORPORATE SPONSORS

 BBC Scotland

 BANK OF SCOTLAND

 KPMG

 ESPC

 navyblue

 BAIRDS fine and country wines

Canon

 ARCAS Computing Ltd.

 pinnacle communications ltd

 STEWARTS

NICHOLAS GROVES RAINES ARCHITECTS

CHAMPAGNE ALAIN THIENOT REIMS - FRANCE

 WIRED NOMAD

ANNIVERSARY ANGELS

 bu edi
A Burrell Company/EDI Group Joint Venture

edNET internetworkingsolutions

 BENNETT & ROBERTSON LLP

 Priority Management Training
People & Projects

 Jean McGhee RECRUITMENT

 Whiteburn projects limited

 BAILLIE GIFFORD

New Horizons Computer Learning Centers Scotland

This theatre has the support of the Pearson Playwright's Scheme sponsored by Pearson plc

The Traverse Trivia Quiz in association with Tennents

With thanks to
Stewarts, printers for the Traverse
Douglas Hall of IMPact Human Resourcing
for management advice arranged through
the Arts & Business skills bank.
Thanks to Claire Aitken of Royal Bank of Scotland
for mentoring support arranged through
the Arts & Business Mentoring Scheme.
Purchase of the Traverse Box Office, computer network
and technical and training equipment
has been made possible with money from
The Scottish Arts Council National Lottery Fund

Scottish
Arts Council
LOTTERY FUNDED

**The Traverse Theatre's work
would not be possible without the support of**

Scottish
Arts Council

·EDINBVRGH·
THE CITY OF EDINBURGH COUNCIL

The Traverse Theatre receives financial assistance from
The Calouste Gulbenkian Foundation, The Peggy Ramsay
Foundation, The Binks Trust, The Bulldog Prinsep Theatrical Fund,
The Esmée Fairbairn Foundation, The Gordon Fraser Charitable
Trust, The Garfield Weston Foundation, The Paul Hamlyn
Foundation, The Craignish Trust, Lindsay's Charitable Trust,
The Tay Charitable Trust, The Ernest Cook Trust, The Wellcome Trust,
The Sir John Fisher Foundation, The Ruben and Elisabeth Rausing
Trust, The Equity Trust Fund, The Cross Trust, N Smith Charitable
Settlement, Douglas Heath Eves Charitable Trust, The Bill and
Margaret Nicol Charitable Trust, The Emile Littler Foundation,
Mrs M Guido's Charitable Trust, Gouvernement du Québec,
The Canadian High Commission

Charity No. SC002368

**For their generous help on
DARK EARTH
the Traverse thanks**

The staff of the Royal Lyceum
The staff of the Quaker Meeting House

Sets, props and costumes for
DARK EARTH
created by Traverse Workshops
(funded by the National Lottery)

 Scottish
Arts Council
LOTTERY FUNDED

Production photography by Douglas Robertson
Print photography by Euan Myles

**For their continued generous support
of Traverse productions the Traverse thanks**

Habitat

Marks and Spencer, Princes Street

Camerabase

BHS

www.traverse.co.uk • www.virtualtraverse.co.uk

TRAVERSE THEATRE – THE COMPANY

David Harrower
Dark Earth

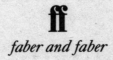

faber and faber

First published in 2003
by Faber and Faber Limited
3 Queen Square London WC1N 3AU
Published in the United States by Faber and Faber Inc.
an affiliate of Farrar, Straus and Giroux LLC, New York

Typeset by Country Setting, Kingsdown, Kent CT14 8ES
Printed in England by Mackays of Chatham plc, Chatham, Kent

The Great Pretender, originally performed by The Platters,
words and music by Buck Ram
© 1955 Panther Music Corp., USA
Peermusic (UK) Ltd., London
Used by permission

A CIP record for this book
is available from the British Library

ISBN 0–571–22170–X

2 4 6 8 10 9 7 5 3 1

Characters

Valerie
woman, thirties

Euan
man, thirties

Petey
farmer, fifties

Ida
his wife, fifties

Christine
their daughter, twenties

On a country road.

In the conservatory of a farmhouse.

In the farmyard.

DARK EARTH

For the Britons, their fears allayed by the absence
of the dreaded legate, began to canvass the woes
of slavery, to compare their wrongs and sharpen
their sting in the telling

Tacitus, *Agricola*

You taught me that like you
I am destitute animal

Paul Durcan, *The Repentant Peter*

DARK EARTH buried soil found in archaeological excavation which often reflects prolonged periods of abandoned settlement; alternatively, deposits of silty soil reworked by earthworms to produce grassland.

A man and a woman are standing on a remote country road.

Euan's holding a map, studying it. Valerie's looking at him.

Valerie Any luck? (*no reply*) Euan?

Euan Mm?

Valerie Have you found us yet?

Euan Trying to. I'm still looking. If this map would fucking work –

Valerie Where's the wall from here? Is it marked on there? Put it down on the ground.

Euan Make it easier, wouldn't it? We're on a fold, I think, if you can believe that. I can't see where –

Valerie Where what?

Euan Where – Cause I can't see where the road goes. Can't see where the road *is*. The D road we're on. The E road we're on. The fucking F, G, H, I road we're on. This goat track of a road.

Valerie We were driving east, weren't we? East /

Euan I should just leave the car there – leave it to rot there, fucking useless piece of junk.

Valerie We've never had a problem with it before.

Euan Unless the petrol gauge is broken, but I filled it, I filled the tank.

Valerie East, and we turned –

Euan And a phone, we have to find a phone now. Wherever a phone's going to be.

Valerie So we must've been heading north. Euan – north?

Euan If they're sending a van out to us, Val, they need to know where we are, not where we were heading.

Valerie I know but they'll – The van'll come from Falkirk, probably, won't it? They'll send it from Falkirk, so whoever's driving the van will probably be a local, won't he? And he'll know where the Antonine Wall is, I should think – it's been there for a while.

Euan There's not even any landmarks. There's nothing to look at, there's nothing to see. We're next to a field of – whatever that is.

Valerie (*checks map*) Passed through Slamannan – not as far as Gardrum Moss. These names – Jawcraig – Cadgersloan –

Euan Somewhere in the middle of there. Stranded on a goat track.

Valerie You said that.

Euan I know. (*short laugh*) Listen how quiet it is.

Valerie Imagine waking up to that. I could wake up to that for a couple of months. (*to herself; looking at her watch*) What time is it?

Euan What do they grow out here? Is there anything to actually eat? Time is it?

Valerie Almost three. There'll be a house or something. A farm.

Euan Maybe even a farmhouse – I better get going.

Valerie Am I not coming with you?

Euan I'm not going to be long.

Valerie You don't know how long you're going to be.

Euan I'll run.

Valerie When do you ever run?

Euan I'll be quicker on my own, Val. I run.

Valerie Alright. (*Beat.*) Two and a half years, I've never seen you run. Go on then. Run.

Euan Give me the map.

Valerie If you don't find anything, don't keep going, alright? Don't keep running. Come back.

Euan We need a phone, Val. I'll keep going until I find one, OK? I'm not going to wait here, not able to do anything, till someone decides to drive past, which could be the middle of next week, couldn't it? Judging by the amount of traffic that thunders past here.

> *Pause.*

Valerie I had other things on my mind, Euan.

Euan It's happened.

Valerie I wanted us to have lunch, a day out together, that's all.

Euan It was the last thing I said.

Valerie Wasn't the last thing.

Euan Have you got my phone? And you shouted you had it. You said –

Valerie I know. I know I did, but I say things sometimes.

Euan I know. I hear you say them. So I tend to believe them.

Valerie Keeps you happy inside your little head, keeps you from moaning. There'll be a house – there'll be a house round that bend there with a phone in every room, a house owned by a retired car mechanic – who had to quit cause – nowadays they don't have the same love, they don't take the same care and pride in the job that he did. Go ask him, he might help.

Euan We might have to forget about Gordon and Ruth's tonight.

Valerie We'll be back by then –! We will!

Euan Who knows how long it's going to take? We're stranded.

Valerie Do I get a last kiss before you start running?

They kiss.

Euan A woman on her own gets priority. In a breakdown. If you phoned them.

Valerie What're you talking about?

Euan They send a van immediately if a woman's on her own.

Valerie I'm not on my own, am I?

Euan Tell them you are. Come with me and tell them you are and I'll hide when they come. I'll hide in the field. Why not? If you want to get /

Valerie Euan, no. Go. Find a phone. Stop talking rubbish.

Euan It's just a thought. It's a way out – it'll take hours off waiting.

Valerie Go. My eyes are closed, my back is turned – run.

Euan leaves.
    She watches him go out of sight. She becomes lost in thought.

An older man enters from the opposite direction:
Petey.

He stops and looks at her. After a moment, she
notices him.

Valerie Hello.

Petey Afternoon.

Valerie looks off in direction Euan went but there's no
sign of him.

Valerie The car's broken down.

Petey That what it is? I was wonderin.

Valerie That's why I'm waiting here. My boyfriend's
gone to look for a phone – two minutes ago.

Petey That way, aye?

Valerie Yeah. (*Pause.*) D'you live around here? D'you –?

Petey That's me headin home the now. Mine'll be the
first house he comes tae less he takes the other road, then
he'll get tae Duncan Craig's.

Valerie How far is it?

Petey Tae mine? No far. Ten, fifteen minutes walkin.
What's he wantin?

Valerie My boyfriend? To use a phone, to –

Petey Get someone out tae you.

Valerie Yeah. So will there be anyone in your house?

Petey Aye, Ida's in. Christine's getting the shoppin. Wife
an daughter. Ida'll sort him out.

Pause. Petey looks towards the car.

Valerie The engine suddenly cut out for no reason.

Petey Cannae be for no reason, must be a reason. Always a reason in there somewhere.

Valerie Yeah. Of course. I didn't /

Petey What're you here for? What're you doin?

Valerie We came for a drive – we're – nothing – just driving. We were looking to have lunch somewhere, then this happened.

Petey Pity. Good car like that dyin on you. (*Pause.*) If I knew anythin about engines I'd be under the bonnet there, takin a look at the fuel pump reset. You from the West are you?

Valerie Yeah –

Petey I've heard talk about it. Gets mentioned sometimes.

Valerie What've you heard?

Petey High opinions o themselves, have they no? High opinions.

Beat.

Valerie It's difficult not to.

Petey I'm sure it's no. Over here for the day.

Valerie That's what we were having trouble with, me and my boyfriend – knowing where we were. Where are we? It's so flat and – featureless, I –

Petey In the middle, that's where you are. Smack in the middle. What our parents always said tae us – this is where you live – smack! (*He mimes a hand slapping.*) – get used tae it. An featureless? You have tae know where tae look.

Valerie Where's the Wall from here? That's where we were going.

Petey You were goin tae the Wall? The Antonine? Where?

Valerie Seabegs Wood? We saw it on the map. I've never been before.

Petey Two miles that way. There's Castlecary an all. An Tamfourhill. But Seabeg's worth a stop. You know about the Romans?

Valerie No, not really, I've never been to the Wall before – we just saw it on the map and thought we'd take a look.

Petey I'd want tae know about the Romans if I knew nothin about them.

Valerie Why? Why's that?

Petey You'll find that out when you know more about them. (*Beat.*) Aye, if I knew more about fan belts I'd definitely be under the bonnet there checkin it's no snapped on you.

Valerie Is there a pub round here I can get a drink while I'm waiting? Is that where you've been?

Petey No the pub. The fountain o youth. It's in a corner there a couple o fields back.

Valerie I should get myself over there.

Petey Help yourself. I'm the only one around here bothers wi it.

   Short pause.

Valerie You going to take a look for me, then?

Petey Aye, I'll take a look-see. Cannae promise much – I havenae my tools and the job might be too big, but aye, I'll look. Nae harm is there?

Valerie Thanks.

Petey What you thankin me for? I've done bugger all yet.

Valerie That's true. I take it back. Let's see what you can do.

Petey You got the keys?

Valerie In the ignition.

Petey You know somethin then.

They walk off to the car.

1.2

Conservatory.
  Euan and Ida.

Ida That you all done?

Euan I think that's it. She'll phone back, she said, if she's any problems.

Ida She's the problem, I'd say. Think she left her brain on the bus goin intae work, that one. How long?

Euan Two hours – two hours plus.

Ida Two hours plus? How's it takin them that long? She say?

Euan Must be busy.

Ida Cannae be that busy. Cup o tea for you there.

Euan No, I should be –

Ida It's made now. Drink it. Aye, sit down.

  He sits.

Euan There must be a lot of call-outs.

Ida Saturday right enough. Aye. Bit stupid-soundin, was she no?

Euan Yeah, maybe a bit.

Ida More than a bit. Saturday girls are always a bit stupid. An where was she? No Scotland.

Euan The command centre'll be in Cardiff or Coventry, somewhere like that. She /

Ida She hadnae a clue. Two hours plus'll be the time it takes her tae find out where she is, where you are an what she's doin wi headphones on.

Euan As long as she passes the directions on.

Ida Wouldnae be too confident o that. I told her tae write down what I was sayin an I don't think she liked that. You've tae do that wi some o them on these phones cause they're no listenin. They've got the hellos and how-can-I-help-yous but they dinnae know how tae listen. If she reads out what she's written the truck'll find us, nae trouble. You don't want tae phone again, speak tae another one?

Euan No, I'll risk it.

Ida More'n likely just as dumb, eh? Saturday girls.

Beat. Euan sips the tea.

Euan You gave her directions to the car, didn't you, not to here?

Ida No. Your car. No good them comin here, is there? It's the top road you've stopped on – it's easy enough tae find. If he comes tae the junction at South Drum he's there, near enough. No far.

Euan Right, I should be off.

Ida What for? See round here, dinnae finish a cup o tea someone's made you, causes offence. True. Seen it happen. Folk harbour it for years.

Euan Then I'll have to be offensive – I don't drink tea. It's coffee I take.

Ida You should've said! I'll make you another one.

Euan No, it doesn't matter, honestly, I'm fine. (*Looks out of the windows behind him.*) And that's all your land out there?

Ida Aye. As far as the eye can see. (*Beat.*) Far as my half-blind eyes can see. Lovely in here though, isn't it, d'you no think? Peaceful.

Euan It is.

Ida I like tae sit in here. D'you like it – in here?

Euan Yeah. Lot of light. Wouldn't be much of a conservatory without that though.

Ida Doesnae need a television, though, I don't think. That would detract, eh? There's magazines tae look at or just tae sit. (*Beat.*) We've a book about the Wall – Aye, we have. On the shelf through there, in the hall, by the phone – I'm sure we've a book.

Euan No – listen –

Ida It'll tell you about it, all you want tae know. You can sit there an have a read o it while you're waitin. You won't be botherin me.

Euan Thanks, Ida, but I have to say no. I need to get back to the car.

Ida People should stay longer when they're here. They should stay an find out what happened, the history. It's all over the place, everywhere you look. It deceives you, this landscape. You'll come back again though, won't you?

Euan I don't know when, but soon.

16

Ida An you'll look in?

Euan I have to get back tonight though – we're going out with some friends – but I'll definitely come again, yeah.

Ida I'm holdin you tae that. Then you'll see all that's here. I won't tell you everythin the now. I'll leave you wonderin so you'll be wantin to come back.

Sound of a car pulling up outside.

Euan Who's that?

Ida That's her now wi the shoppin. Christine. My daughter.

Euan I'm off then.

Ida Stay there. She'll give you a lift back up the road.

Euan No, I –

Ida (*going out*) Stay.

Ida leaves.
Euan waits. He looks at the conservatory door, goes over to it. He tries the handle. The door's locked but the key's there. He turns it.
Christine has appeared at the doorway into the house. She's watching him.
Euan turns and sees her.

Euan Hello.

She's staring at him.

Christine Who're you?

Euan Euan.

Christine Euan? How are you?

Euan Fine. I'm good.

Christine An is that you sneakin out the back door, Euan?

Euan (*smiles*) I didn't want to bother you /

Christine Did she tell you tae go, Euan, did she? Double quick? An where's your car? Didnae see it in the yard – you hidden it?

Euan Hidden it? I don't know what you're – I –

Christine You werenae quick enough, were you?

Euan I'm going back to my car now.

Christine What bank you from?

Ida's in the doorway.

Ida He's no from any bank, you. What you talkin about?

Christine (*to Ida*) What you doin?

Euan I'm not from a bank –

Ida Dinnae listen tae her.

Christine What's he doin here then?

Ida The welcome! D'you hear that? He's a guest in our home.

Euan My car's broken down /

Ida Up on the top road.

Christine Kinda car is it?

Ida He doesnae have tae answer that –!

Euan It's a /

Christine You tellin me the truth?

Euan I /

Ida Give the man a chance tae speak! (*to Euan*) Let her settle. Dinnae rise tae it. Chargin in, no even interested in explanation. An his name's Euan.

Christine Aye, I got that.

Ida This's the daughter I should have warned you about: Christine.

Christine Pleased tae meet you.

They shake hands.

Euan Do I really look like I'm from a bank?

Christine Could be.

Euan You're joking. Not any bank I go to.

Christine They get them tae dress casual now. So they're less o a threat. So's the likes o us identify wi them. An you did look like you were sneakin out the back door.

Euan Is /

Ida That is no the back door!

Christine What is it then? What would you call the door out tae the back?

Ida The conservatory door.

Christine Conservatory door –! (*to Euan*) Cause you're here we're gettin this.

Ida We didnae pay all that money for you tae call it the back door. And it's no cause o him! Go and make a cup o tea, somethin useful. An bring through the Tunnocks wafers you've probably no bought tae spite me.

Christine Twelve for the price o ten. They're sittin in the bag through there.

Euan It was nice to meet you. I have to get going. Thanks for letting me use the phone. I'm sorry for disturbing you.

Christine Needs more'n that tae disturb anythin here.

Ida You're a distraction.

Christine You'll be a topic o interest for the next couple o days at least, Euan – how's that feel?

Ida I said you'd give him a lift back up the road.

Christine Give me a minute.

Euan It doesn't matter.

Christine I'll take you but I'm just in the door. Did you pay for the use o the phone?

Euan Oh. Yeah. I –

Ida She's jokin, Euan. Put it away. I'll go make some tea – coffee.

Euan Really, I don't want any coffee.

Ida But you didn't drink your tea. Two hours plus he's havin tae wait for them tae get here an fix his car.

Christine What's up wi it?

Euan Nothing that can't be fixed in five minutes, I hope. I haven't a clue. I'm useless with engines.

Christine My dad knows about engines – maybe he'll take a look.

Ida He's gone out for a walk.

Christine glances at Ida.

Euan here was goin tae the Wall.

Euan I've been going to the wall for years –

Beat.

Ida (*not understanding*) Years –? But you said you'd never been?

Christine Joke, Mum. People who work in banks have a strange sense o humour.

Ida Was it? I meant the Antonine Wall – that's where you were goin. That's where he was goin.

Christine Is that where you were goin, aye?

Euan Yeah. Just going to have a look.

Christine Wouldnae bother. It's no worth it.

Euan Is it not?

Ida Course it is!

Christine So worth it she's never been.

Ida I've been. Course I've been. It's on our doorstep.

Christine Step out the door an walk two miles that way.

Ida An you havenae been in a good few years.

Christine Back where we started. Cause it's no worth the bother. It'd drown you, Euan, the treacherous depths o the conversation we have in here sometimes.

Ida Showin off.

Christine I'm no showin off!

Ida This is the one, Euan, begged tae go there every weekend when she was wee.

Christine Begged –?

Ida Couldnae get enough o the place.

Christine Dragged by my dad.

Euan There's something there, though. There's still something to see. There's still ruins, isn't there?

Christine If you count ruins as a kind o misshapen ugly lump on the ground.

Ida She used tae love it there. Every weekend, I'm tellin you.

Christine An no even an impressive much o a lump. Go tae Hadrian's – it's miles better. You'll get a wall that looks like a wall. An experience.

Ida He's come here, though. Wantin tae see the Antonine. He's interested.

Christine Are you? You interested? He's no interested.

Euan Yeah, I am.

Ida I was tellin him you've a book on it – out in the hall, isn't it, on the shelf there?

Christine Very thin book. You wouldnae get tired o callin it a pamphlet even.

Ida Go and get it for him then. You know where it is.

Christine He's no wantin tae read that. Are you?

Euan No. No, I'm not. I don't have time.

Ida She used tae be intae all that in a big way.

Christine What's 'all that'? 'All that in a big way'? Latin'd be easier sometimes.

Ida The Romans. All that. All that went on here. There's more. She knows all about it.

Christine Leave it – he's burstin tae get goin, look at him.

Ida Prince Charlie. Tell him. Bonnie Prince Charlie. Marchin right through here intae Edinburgh, didn't he? Right past here, right past us. Didn't he, Christine? Tell the man.

Christine C'mon, I'll take you back.

Ida She doesnae want tae talk about it. Keeps it all tae herself.

Christine Best place for it.

Ida A lot went on here, Euan. But you wouldnae know it if you didnae know it. That's why you tell other people, Christine. So they know too. Makes the place come alive for them.

Christine A'right. Enough.

Ida An other people tell other people an it gets passed around. Shared. What's wrong wi that?

Christine Nothin's wrong wi that. Nothin. But now's no the time an Euan's wantin his life back. You comin?

Ida Wait – I'll write down our number for you.

Christine What for?

Ida In case. (*Ida goes out.*)

Christine In case? In case o what? No plannin on rushin back here, are you?

Euan So d'you work on the farm, do you?

Christine No.

Euan I don't work in a bank and you don't work on the farm. We got there in the end.

Christine Where you goin back tae?

Euan Glasgow.

Christine That a Glasgow accent?

Euan It's my Glasgow accent.

Christine You've a good voice – I like it. This is stupid. You don't need our phone number, you're not goin tae phone us. C'mon.

She walks towards the conservatory door. Euan follows. He moves oddly suddenly, stops, holding one arm close to his body.

What's wrong?

23

Euan Nothing.

Christine What is it?

Short pause.

Euan I get this pain sometimes. It's nothing.

Christine Doesnae look like nothin. What's the matter wi you?

Euan Christine –

Christine What?

She moves towards him. As she does, something falls from inside his jacket onto the floor.
Christine looks at it. It's her book about the Antonine Wall.

That's my book. (*She picks it up.*) This's my book. Were you stealin it? Were you nickin this from me? Were you?

Euan I don't know why I did it. I –

Christine You don't know why you were nickin it?

Euan I'm sorry I'm – I don't know what to say.

Christine An it's been under your jacket all this time –? I don't believe this! I don't fuckin believe this! An you were goin tae walk straight out the door wi it?

Euan I'm sorry.

Christine You tried tae nick a book I've had since I was seven years old!

Euan I took it for my girlfriend.

Christine Your girlfriend –! Where? What girlfriend?

Euan She's back at the car. She's waiting in the car.

Christine You think I'm soft in the head or somethin? You're makin this up.

Euan No, she is. She's there.

Christine What the fuck do I care? You were takin this for her?

Beat.

Euan Things aren't very good between us right now.

Christine An you thought a book on Roman ruins would get things goin again?

Euan I thought – She was interested in seeing the Wall as well. I – It was a spur of the moment thing. A fucking stupid thing to do.

Pause.

Christine You left her in the car waitin for you?

Euan Yeah.

Christine Still don't believe you.

Euan I'll just go.

Christine Aye. I would. (*She points to the house door.*) Through the house gets you ontae the road and away from here quicker.

Ida re-enters, holding out a piece of paper.

Ida There you go – phone number an address. (*She sees the book.*) Is that it? That's the book I was tellin him about, isn't it?

Christine Aye, it is. It's the book. The very one.

Ida Well, are you lettin him have a look or no?

Euan I'm going, Ida. Thank you. (*He moves towards the house door.*)

Ida You no takin him?

Euan No, I want to walk.

He exits.
   Ida looks at Christine.

Christine I'm goin upstairs. (*Christine exits into the house.*)

Ida Euan – the phone number –!

Ida exits into the house.
   Some moments pass.
   Petey enters by the conservatory door.

Petey Ida? Ida!

Valerie enters.

She's no here. No one's here. Sit down. She won't have got far. She never makes it over the perimeter fence. Doesnae stop her tryin though.

Valerie It's lovely in here. The fields out the back. It's really lovely. So bright.

Petey Aye. We had it built – when? Eighty-nine abouts. Good old days.

Valerie Have you lived here long?

Petey Life sentence. Every one o the fifty-three years.

Valerie Are you the son of a son of a son then?

Petey Always been told I'm a son of a something – never caught the last word though. Aye, my father was here tae. House's always been dark inside – it's why we built this on, the south side. Tae harness the light, y'know?

Valerie Harness the light. That's a lovely expression.

Petey We're like that here. Poetry flyin off our tongues like shit off a shovel.

Valerie I can hear.

Petey It's unique though, the light. Never seen it anywhere else. Some o the days you get here – how the sun
is. You're puttin off the time till you have tae walk back
intae the burial chamber there.

Valerie Where's Christine? Is she around? I'd like to meet
her.

Petey She must be. She should be back by now.

Ida appears at the door.

Ida It's you.

Petey Aye.

Ida (*to Valerie*) Hello.

Petey Found her on the top road, broken down.

Valerie Hi. I'm Valerie.

Ida The Drum road?

Valerie I don't know. Is it?

Petey She's wantin to find out was her fella here usin the
phone?

Ida Euan?

Valerie He's been here? Has he gone?

Ida Never mentioned a girl. Are you wi him?

Petey She's been up at the car waitin on him.

Ida He never said anythin about it.

Valerie Has he gone?

Ida A minute ago. Wait an I'll fetch him back.

Ida goes out.
  A short silence between Petey and Valerie.
  Petey's staring at Christine's book. He picks it up.

Petey What's this doin out?

Valerie What is it?

Petey hands her the book.

Petey Christine hasnae looked at that in a long while.

Valerie opens the book.

Valerie 'Christine Cauldwell. My dad gave me this book. November 1990.'

Valerie begins looking through the book.
Ida re-enters with Euan.

Ida I got him for you.

Euan What're you here for? (*Euan sees she's holding the book.*)

Valerie I met Petey.

Petey Hello.

Ida (*to Petey*) This is Euan.

Valerie It's the clutch cable, Euan, it's broken. Clutch cable which is attached to the clutch fork.

Petey An whoever's comin out'll have a repair kit – metal toggle kind o thing that'll hold it for the now.

Euan Right. OK. Good. Thanks.

Ida You never said anythin about a girlfriend.

Euan Well, this is her. Valerie. My girlfriend. I was just heading back.

Valerie Good, cause I was getting tired of waiting.

Petey You wantin somethin tae drink, Val?

Euan glances at Petey.
Valerie's looking at Euan.

Euan No, we should start walking back – shouldn't we, Val?

Ida Euan, tell her the truth –! They're goin tae be about two hours.

Valerie Two hours –!

Euan It'll be less than that now.

Ida Two hours plus, the girl said. So you've time for a cup o tea.

Valerie OK. Yeah, I will. Thanks. Milk and sugar.

Euan No, Valerie, we should go –

Petey Why no wait here, the two o you?

Ida Aye. Wait. You'll no be botherin us.

Euan No, we can't. We have to get back to the car.

Valerie I'm not going to sit in a car for two hours –!

Ida When she could be sittin in here, drinkin a cup o tea and a Tunnock's wafer that Christine remembered to buy, miracle o miracles.

Euan No, we have to go, they could be –

Christine has appeared in the doorway.

Petey Christine, there you are.

Christine What's goin on?

Ida Euan's got a girlfriend.

Valerie Hello. I'm Valerie.

Petey This is my daughter, Christine. I found her on the top road.

Christine I was wantin tae meet you – Euan was talkin about you.

Ida No tae me.

Christine (*to Valerie*) Cannae believe he left you on your own.

Ida (*to Euan*) You ashamed o her or somethin?

Valerie Are you? Is that what it is? The truth finally.

Euan Valerie, can we just go, please. Now.

Petey You don't have tae.

Valerie (*holds up the book*) I'm looking at this.

Petey (*to Christine*) Why've you brought that out, Christine?

Christine It wasn't me. (*Beat.*) It was Mum. She wanted Euan tae look at it.

Petey That's where you were headin, wasn't it?

Euan Yeah.

Valerie I've never been before.

Euan It's not worth it.

Ida Aye, course it is. Dinnae listen tae this one. Milk and sugar, Valerie. What's in yours, Euan? I'm no forgettin it's coffee.

Christine Are they stayin?

Ida Aye, they're stayin.

Christine Are they? Thought you were wantin tae get off quick like.

Valerie It is alright, are you sure?

Petey Aye, course it is. Till the truck comes, Christine.

Euan I want to go, Valerie. Now. I mean it. Now.

Valerie Go then. I'm happy here. And I need a cup of tea because I'm dying of thirst. I'll see you back at the car in two hours.

Ida Two hours plus. Euan, get on the phone tae them, speak tae them, tell them tae send the truck here.

Valerie Why not, Euan? I don't see what difference it makes.

Christine An you'll be more comfortable sittin here, d'you no think?

Ida Petey, you come an give the girl directions. I've tried once already.

> *Ida goes out.*
> *Euan looks over at Valerie, as Petey leaves. She's looking at the book again. Euan goes out.*
> *Valerie and Christine left together.*

Valerie We only came out for a drive – I said to him why don't we go out for a drive and neither of us had ever driven here before even though it's so close – we don't even know what it looks like – and we were going to stop and have lunch somewhere, I don't know where, find somewhere – then it was past three and they usually stop serving lunch after three so – And I'd seen a sign earlier for the Wall near Greenhill.

Christine Seabegs Wood.

Valerie So we decided to drive back that way to have a look at it and then the car died on us.

Christine Outside Falkirk's better. Rough Castle.

Valerie Oh, right. Right, we'll go there next time then.

Christine But even that's no very good. People always leave sayin how disappointed they are.

Pause. Valerie holds up the book.

Valerie Do you mind if I –?

Christine No. Go ahead. My dad gave me that when I was a girl.

Valerie I saw that. Inside the front cover. Christine Cauldwell.

Christine Aye. That's me.

> *Valerie opens the book, begins to read.*
> *Christine watches her.*

1.3

Conservatory. Early evening.
> *Valerie sits reading the book. Euan just sitting.*

Euan What's it sayin then?

Valerie Mm? Quite a lot.

Euan You going to keep reading it?

Valerie I think so. I'm interested.

Euan What's that look for? You haven't looked at me for the last few hours, you haven't said a word in my direction so I can tell a look like that one.

Valerie Did you have to eat so much?

> *He's taken aback.*

Three whole plates of it.

Euan I was hungry –! They invited us – Ida invited us to eat.

Valerie Never seen you eat as fast as that. Wasn't eating, it was wolfing. You were wolfing it down you.

Euan It was good and she kept offering me more so I kept saying yes.

Valerie It was embarrassing.

Euan You were the only person who thought that. Ida and Petey didn't. (*Beat.*) This is cause I didn't mention you to them, isn't it?

Valerie Struck me as a bit strange, yeah.

Euan I was trying to get away. I was trying to leave.

Valerie You sat and had a cup of coffee, she told me.

Euan I didn't have a cup of coffee – I had a cup of tea –

Valerie You don't drink tea.

Euan You've seen them – you've heard how they talk – If I'd told them about you back at the car I'd never have got out of here.

Valerie You haven't got out. You're still here. (*Beat.*) I should be in your thoughts at all times.

Euan You are.

Valerie Day and night. I should be implanted in your frontal lobe.

Euan Can I come over there?

Valerie No –

> *He begins to move towards her. Off his seat towards her in hers.*
> *Christine has appeared in the doorway.*

Stay away from me.

> *They now see her. Euan's caught midway. He moves back to his seat.*

Hello, Christine.

Christine She fed you as well, did she?

Valerie Yeah. It was delicious.

Christine An now she's wantin tae know if you're wantin coffee or tea?

Euan Nothing for me, thanks.

Valerie No thanks.

Christine Well, if you change your mind don't be afraid tae go in and help yourself.

Valerie You off out tonight then?

Christine Dunno. Haven't decided yet. How long the two o you been together then?

Valerie Two and a half years.

Christine An how is it? Goin together that long? I've never done it.

Valerie It's good.

Euan Yeah.

Christine Mm, must try it by the sound o it. Is this the longest you've been out wi anybody?

Valerie Not me, no. I was with somebody else for about five years – and then that ended. And about a year later I met Euan.

Euan What about you? You got a boyfriend?

Christine Me? No. I'm out on my own.

Valerie (*smiles*) That's a good way to be.

Christine I know.

    Ida enters with Petey.

Ida (*to Christine*) You asked them?

34

Christine Naw, they don't want anythin.

Ida Cause you didnae ask them. You /

Euan She did, Ida. We don't want anything.

Ida Sure, the both o you?

Valerie Yeah. Thanks, Ida. That was lovely. You shouldn't've but –

Ida You should've had more. You didnae eat much. I didnae think you liked it.

Petey You no hungry, Christine?

Christine No really.

Euan gets to his feet.

Euan I – I should try again, shouldn't I? Phoning them. Find out where the hell he is, this mechanic.

Christine Many times is that now?

Valerie Too many. I'm sorry about this.

Christine Just askin – cause this seems to be one hell o an amateur operation, does it no?

Euan He's got our number – he's got this number. He should've phoned by now to tell us where he is. He's been given the directions.

Petey Aye, I gave them directions right tae the door.

Euan I'll find out what's going on. I'll talk to the manager or something, whoever's in charge.

Ida On you go, son. Lay down the law.

Valerie We'll pay for this – we're paying for all the calls.

Ida Dinnae worry about that the now.

Euan goes through into the house.

Christine Thought you'd carry mobiles wi you – successful people like yourselves, naw?

Valerie It's my fault. I left them at home.

Christine His as well?

Valerie I was meant to put them in my bag but I forgot – my mind was on other things.

Ida We have them, don't we?

Christine Dinnae use them really.

Petey Speak tae each other enough as it is.

Christine moves towards the conservatory door.

Ida Where you goin?

Christine To stand shiverin outside in the cold. A cigarette's needin smoked.

Christine leaves.
    Valerie's left with Ida and Petey.

Ida Don't like anyone smokin in here.

Petey If you're no havin a drink, Val, how bout havin a drink?

Valerie What kind of drink are you talking about?

Petey The only decent kind – the water o life.

Valerie Malt whisky?

Petey Of course, malt whisky. From some uninhabited, broke-down island or other, over your way. Will you have one?

Ida Course she will.

Petey An you dinnae need tae be asked.

Ida I never need tae be asked. I'll get the ice.

36

Ida leaves.
Petey brings out the whisky bottle and three glasses.

Petey Bunnahabhain. Islay. Where's that? Who cares? Long as they get it tae the mainland in their rowboats safe. What would you live on an island for? (*He pours the whisky.*) It was built o turf an timber.

Valerie What was?

Petey The Wall. Built wi turf an timber.

Valerie Is that unusual? I don't –

Petey Considerin Hadrian's Wall was made wi stone, aye. Some'll tell you it was made o turf cause it was temporary, a rush job thrown up quick tae repel the northern hordes – but they're wrong. The Antonine was up-tae-the-minute – a pinnacle o Roman field-engineerin. It was. It was a statement, Val, the edge o their magnificent empire reached tae here. On our doorstep almost. If you dug down right under where we are, under the topsoil, you'd see. Centimetres – centimetres! – are a thousand years, did you know that?

Valerie And what –

Petey You'd find all kind o stuff, diggin down. Pottery and coins and glass. Aw, they're no far away, the Romans.

Valerie It's incredible, isn't it?

Petey That's a good enough word for what it is, Val, aye – incredible.

Valerie And what about you, Petey?

Petey Me? Where do I come intae this?

Valerie You live here. You know this place. Your family's been here – what is it? – sixty, seventy years –?

Petey Aye.

Valerie You're still working hard – you're still /

Petey Hard, you're sayin tae me? Hard. You'd never guess, Valerie. Aye, it's hard.

Ida enters.

The hardest it's ever been.

Ida What're you talkin about, you? I thought you were goin tae tell her all about the Wall an everythin?

Petey She started askin me about the farm.

Ida The farm's the least o it, Val. We're surrounded by it, Val. History's lyin around everywhere you step. Comin back in, wipin your shoes you're wipin off –

Euan appears in the doorway.

What'd they say?

Short pause.

Euan The van's gone back. The guy's gone home. The f –

Petey Bugger.

Euan – 's gone home.

Valerie Why didn't he phone?

Euan (*shrugs*) They don't know why.

Ida Same lassie?

Euan The same lassie. This guy they were sending's not part of them directly, they subcontract him, they – I don't know what they do – they make up excuses, they piss me off, I'll wring someone's neck, I'll – is that whisky?

Beat.

Petey Where?

Euan There.

Petey Aye. Aye it is. So what're you goin tae do now then?

Valerie's laughing.

Ida Give him a glass –! He's only jokin wi you, Euan. Give him a glass.

Petey gets Euan a glass, pours it.

Valerie What are we going to do?

Ida You're fine there the now.

Petey hands him a whisky.

Euan We'll have to get a taxi. Thanks. (*Euan takes a drink from the glass.*)

Ida Much is that goin tae cost?

Petey Fair amount, I'd guess. Region o forty, fifty, sixty.

Valerie It doesn't matter.

Euan drains his glass in the second gulp.

Ida That's what we want tae see!

Euan We have to, don't we? We've no choice. It's the only thing we can do. D'you have a number for a taxi firm?

Petey There'll be one in the book. Falkirk. We dinnae use taxis much.

Euan (*to Valerie*) Will you phone a taxi?

Valerie Yeah. If you want. Can I finish this first?

Euan Yeah – course.

Ida Petey'll do it for you.

Petey I'll do it, aye.

Euan Then I'll have to get another one back out here in the morning.

This is directed to Valerie but she's looking at Petey.

Valerie I can't believe he's gone home.

Petey He can't have tried very hard.

Ida It's cause we're so secluded here, eh, Petey? Private an secluded an peaceful. Look at you there, Val. You havenae been so relaxed in months, I bet, have you?

Valerie You might be right, Ida, aye.

Euan looks at Valerie.

What?

Petey You said aye.

Valerie Did I?

Ida You did, aye.

Euan I'm going outside to get some air.

Valerie Did I? I didn't even notice.

Ida Country air out there, Euan. Gulp it down. You'll feel a world o difference. An just think o the people who've breathed it up the centuries.

Euan Right. I will. I'll keep that in mind.

He exits by conservatory door.
Short pause.

Ida Private an peaceful an relaxin.

Valerie We're always talking about getting away for the weekends but we never do, we never get round to it. I'll have to start forcing him. It is peaceful – I am relaxed. Might fall asleep here.

Petey You won't be used tae that, will you, Val? Peace an quiet – livin across there in that swamp.

Valerie Swamp? Is that what you think o us?

Petey Naw. It's geography.

Ida We're up high here – the water drains down either side. East an west. You get our slops.

Petey The glacial shelf, Val, that's what it is. Nothin can be done about it.

Ida What's it you do, Val?

Valerie Liaison manager. For a company in Glasgow. I love it.

Petey I probably would tae if I knew what it was.

Ida Meetin people, isn't it? Seein tae their needs.

Valerie That's one part of it. Not sure what the other parts are, but who cares?

Petey Is liaisin no meetin people in secret? Is that what you do? You a spy, Val? You here spyin on us?

Valerie No. They told me I was to deny everything. So no.

Ida But you'll say aye tae another drink?

Valerie Aye. Fill her up, captain.

Ida (*laughs*) Captain –

Petey Will do.

Valerie I don't get this kind of attention in my own home.

Ida It's just our way. We dinnae even notice.

Valerie Cheers. Thanks for having us here.

Ida Cheers.

Petey Cheers.

Valerie Here's to you.

Petey Here's tae us.

Ida Here's tae us meetin you.

They drink.

Outside, in the yard, the security light goes on. It's a harsh light. Euan holds his hand up to his eyes. Christine's smoking a fag.

Euan It's bright, isn't it?

Christine Supposed tae be – it's tae warn off intruders an petty thieves. What you wantin out here?

Euan We're getting a taxi back.

Christine Why should I be bothered? (*Beat.*) Taxi? That'll cost you. Expensive wee run out tae the country for you an the girl, eh? Is that it? Comin out tae tell me somethin I didnae need tae know but got a laugh out o anyway.

Euan Thanks for – not saying anything. I appreciate it.

Christine Be in some shit if I had, wouldn't you? Naw, wee bit o squirmin goes a long way. Had that book since I was seven years old. *The Antonine Wall* by A. S. Robertson, third edition. Hard tae get hold of nowadays. Well, no for some.

Euan It was a stupid thing to do – a fucking unbelievably stupid thing to do and I'm sorry. I don't know what made me do it.

Christine Pure instinct, it was, made you do it. I'm havin that, thank you very much.

Euan No, it wasn't like that. I'm not like that.

Christine So you'd a wee think about it first? While you were speakin on our phone my mother let you use for free. Diggin yourself deeper here, are you no?

Euan I don't go around stealing things like that.

Christine An what would you have told her when she opened it an saw another woman's name there? That I'd love tae see.

    Beat.

Euan I'd have told her I bought it in a second-hand shop.

Christine I think you're sleekit, are you? That's the opinion I'm forming. Sleekit an sly maybe. Are you? Is that what's up between you? – She cannae trust you?

Euan That's none o your business.

Christine You made it my business by usin it as an excuse – though maybe it's no an excuse the way it was goin on wi the two o you in there. Maybe that's all she wants tae do. Trust you. An what do you do? Go an nick a book for her.

Euan I'm not going to talk about my girlfriend with you. I did a fucking mad stupid thing, alright? A fucking mad stupid out-of-character thing. You never done anything like that? No, probably not.

Christine And you'll know the kind o person I am after knowin me all this time? I might've. I was goin tae run away once – probably a mad fuckin stupid thing *no* tae do. Give me time. Give me time till I'm somewhere near approachin your age.

Euan Why did you want to run away?

Christine Doesnae matter now. I stayed.

Euan How old are you?

Christine Why? Twenty.

Euan Only twenty? You seem older.

Christine Feel twice that sometimes. No sure if I've grown up too quick or stayed young too long. Maybe both at the same time. Aye, half of me's only twenty.

Euan And you said you don't work on the farm, so what d'you do out here?

Christine What're you so interested for?

Euan I'm interested. What keeps you here? What keeps a twenty-year-old girl here?

Christine I live here. Is that no enough? It's enough for me. (*Pause.*) Least I know where I am an how tae get out. You dinnae even know that. You're lost. So dinnae speak without knowin what you're speakin about – cause you don't know the first thing about this place.

Euan No, you keep all that to yourself, don't you? Your mother was trying to prise it out of you.

Christine She'd need a crowbar.

Euan So what you going to do with all that knowledge? Tell it to the cows?

Christine Fair got the bit between your mouth now, haven't you?

Euan Are you going to go to college?

Christine It was you in the dock a minute ago – how's it turned so quick? See, I was right – sly, sleekit. College? Why no university? I could go tae university. I might be goin for all you know. You'll have went, won't you? You've got that look.

Euan Yeah. I went.

Christine Well, I'm no goin anywhere. School was torture enough. Why'd I want tae prolong the pain o that? They'd never give you a chance to learn what you really wanted tae. Sit an listen tae all kinds o subjects I couldnae give a toss about and then they couldnae understand me wantin to know everythin I could about what really interested me. Where I live. Round here. I know all about round here. All there is tae know. I'd tae learn most of it myself cause with them it was always, right, we need tae move on now but I never wanted tae. I know about the Romans an their empire an Agricola an Antoninus an the Votadini and the Selgovae. I know about Charlie an the seven men o Moidart an the genius Lord George Murray an old Jamie the Rover bidin his time in Rome. I know more people from round here joined him than any o them fuckin Highlanders. You don't know any o that, do you? Or about dairy herds and set-aside and cereal prices. I know about where I live.

Euan You're right. You're better off here.

Christine How? What's that mean? Dinnae patronise.

Euan I'm not.

Christine You are.

Euan I've forgotten most of what I used to know. I've forgotten what I studied. What degree I got. It's all gone. I'm serious. The brain hardens, Christine – things just bounce back off it. I'm not patronising you.

Christine So you won't know why your girlfriend sits in there an says, 'Stay away from me'?

Euan (*short laugh*) Fuck. You miss nothing, do you?

Christine Try not tae.

Euan She didn't mean it.

Christine Did she no?

Euan We say these – (*His eyes close.*)

Christine What's wrong wi you?

Euan Pain in my chest.

Christine No another one? I'm no goin tae have tae search you again, am I?

Euan It's indigestion. It's nothing.

Christine Massage it. The middle o your chest. There.

Euan Here?

Christine Aye.

Pause. He massages his chest.

Euan I was saying we say things like that to each other. You'll learn about that.

Christine Will I? Cause here we just up and say what we mean. Tell me again, what you were doin drivin out here?

Euan Just driving. Day out.

Christine An whose idea was it?

Euan It was hers.

Inside a voice has begun singing. It's Ida.

Is that your mother singing?

They listen.

Christine Aw naw. What's this for?

But she goes quiet, listens for a moment. They both do.

Euan Why did you think I was from a bank?

Christine Cause we're rakin it in so much workin a small family farm they're always on at us tae invest wi them –

but see, us, we're strictly under-the-mattress people. Oh, shouldnae be tellin you that, should I? (*Pause.*) An she forgot tae bring her mobile an your mobile?

Euan Yeah.

Christine Just forgot. (*Beat.*) Cause if it was me, I'd be wonderin tae myself. I'd be wonderin.

> *Pause.*

No, I cannae listen tae this. I cannae listen tae this, I'm sorry.

> *Christine walks off.*
> *After a moment, Euan follows.*
> *In the conservatory, Ida finishes her song.*
> *Christine and Euan enter. Euan sits down, still feeling the pain of his indigestion.*

Valerie That was beautiful.

Petey That was always the song she'd sing.

Ida Come'n sit down, Euan. You get all the air you wanted?

Euan Yeah.

Valerie You alright?

Euan Yeah.

Ida Look at her standin there embarrassed.

Christine No, I'm no.

Ida Embarassed at her old mother openin her mouth for a song.

Christine Just wonderin what the occasion is.

Ida No occasion. Does there have tae be an occasion?

Christine For you tae sing, aye.

Petey Saturday night, Christine. That's the occasion.

Ida Neighbours'd be round here, Saturday nights, or we'd be round theirs, the room'd be full and there'd always be singin. Everyone took a turn. Everyone had a song.

Valerie Did they?

Christine Telly and satellite killed all that. Thank God.

Ida We'd have some nights, eh, Petey? Some nights willnae be forgotten.

Petey Aye. There were a few.

Christine Sounds wild, doesn't it? Singsongs an whisky intae the night. Naw. In bed by ten. Always.

Valerie Ten?

Ida Had tae be.

Petey Farmers' hours. Couldnae keep our eyes open past then.

Ida No use feelin useless the next day, nae use tae anyone.

Christine Cept for that one night, remember?

Ida No.

Christine Aye, you do.

Euan What night?

Christine The night they didnae come back by ten – that dark, dark night –

Ida What're you sayin? They dinnae want tae hear that.

Valerie I do.

Petey Listen.

Christine Age fourteen, I'm sittin here on my own wonderin what's happened, if they've crashed, or the house they're at –

Ida Duncan an Susannah.

Christine – has burnt down or – all manner o things – cause they're always in bed by ten nae matter what.

Petey Poor lassie on her own. We hadnae phoned or anythin –

Christine An it's ten tae eleven now and I'm sat through there in the kitchen watchin the clock, waitin till exactly eleven cause I wasnae goin tae pick up that phone a second before. Know how children can be like that?

Valerie Yeah.

Ida Only you. She'd have been havin the time o her life, whole house tae herself.

Christine An I phone an it rings an it rings – an it rings – nae answer machines then – an it rings –

Petey Get on wi it, Jackanory.

Christine An finally it's picked up an a voice is on the other end. 'Hello?'

Ida Susannah, the wife.

Christine 'Hello?' Like I just got her out o bed or somethin. An I says tae her – where's my mum and dad? Where are they?

Ida Abrupt even then. Nae pleasantries tae speak o.

Christine An I hear her goin, 'Ida . . . Ida . . .' An then it's her. Groanin.

Ida Groanin –!

Christine groans.

No, I wasnae. No like that.

Christine An I'm thinkin what's goin on, what the hell's goin on here?

49

Petey They had parties like that in the seventies. I'm told.

Christine This wasnae the seventies – what you talkin about?

Petey No. No, it wasnae, was it?

Christine groans again.

Ida Stop it, you!

Christine Just like that. And I can hear the telly goin in the background an then her voice. 'Is that you, Christine?'

Ida Alky I'm soundin now.

Christine She'd just woken up. They'd all fallen asleep –

Valerie All of them?

Christine All four o them – grown adults – crashed out durin one o their rousin singsongs.

Petey Been there till mornin if she hadnae phoned.

Christine Four o them crashed out like that.

Ida All I remember's comin in the back door –

Christine The conservatory door.

Ida An she's sittin there where she is now, lookin at us, disapprovin. Shakin your head.

Christine Never lost that. Still dae it.

Ida Your own daughter shakin her head at you. Imagine the shame.

Christine Still find reasons tae.

Ida Could've been my mother sittin there shakin her head at me comin back from bein late out.

Christine An here's me thinkin I'd gotten out the genetic curse tae.

Petey She was that grown-up we didnae have any worries, did we, Christine?

Ida Always used tae laugh – always said Christine arranged her own birth. Petey an me just did what we were told. Ran like clockwork as well.

Christine Shut up, you. I was fourteen, in the house on my own. Abandoned, deserted by my own mother an father.

Ida Things havenae changed much. Still stuck wi you here on a Saturday night.

Christine Thanks very much, darlin mother o mine.

Euan looks at Christine, who knows he's looking. Pause.

Petey Christine used tae love the singin before she stopped it.

Valerie Did you?

Ida Aye, she did.

Christine Conversation's endin now. I'd be wonderin about him.

All look at Euan.

Ida What's wrong wi him?

Valerie (*to Euan*) What's wrong with you? You're hardly sayin a word.

Euan We should be goin. When's the taxi coming?

Christine It's indigestion.

Valerie Is it?

Christine I'll see if we've got anythin for it. Keep massagin it like I showed you.

Valerie glances at Christine, then at Euan.
  Christine goes out.

Ida Lie back, Euan. Sit round. That's it. You want tae be more horizontal.

Valerie Wonder why this's come on?

Ida Hope it wasnae my food.

Euan (*shakes his head*) No. It wasn't the food.

Valerie It was how he ate the food, Ida.

Ida How did he eat the food? Put the fork tae his mouth like all o us, did you no?

Euan That's exactly what I did, yeah.

Petey There was the one we used tae sing, Ida.

Ida Who?

Petey Me an Christine.

Ida Aw – Aye.

Valerie What was it?

Petey Somethin she made up.

Ida Give it a go. See what happens.

Petey Naw.

Ida Go on.

Valerie Please –

  Christine re-enters carrying a glass of water.

Christine Cannae find anythin for it. This'll have tae do.

Petey (*sings*)
  Oh yes I'm –

Christine Aw nawww – Should've fuckin seen this comin –

Ida Oi, you! Language in the conservatory!

Christine I'm no listenin.

Ida They used tae do it together, the two o them.

Christine There's a man dyin here.

Valerie Leave him. He'll be fine.

Ida She wrote it. Only she could've written it.

Christine I didnae write it! What're you talkin about?
The stuff that comes out their mouths! The world you
live in.

Ida Same as yours, Christine.

Petey Twelve years old she was, up on her feet, beltin it
out.

Christine I'm goin tae my room – nailin the door shut –
diggin a tunnel oot o here.

Valerie Sing it. Please. I'd love to hear it.

Petey sings to the tune of 'The Great Pretender'.

Petey
Oh yes –

Christine Walkin out o here –

Petey Just for tonight, Christine. Go on. *I'm the –*

Valerie Go on, Christine. Let's hear it.

Ida Out wi it.

Petey It's the last time I'll ever ask you.

Christine looks at him.

Euan Go on, Christine.

Christine Only if you sing as well. The both o you. Fair's
fair.

Euan I don't know any songs.

Valerie I'll sing one – I don't know what, but I'll sing one.

Petey
Oh yes I'm the –

They all look at Christine. Pause.

Christine
– Young Pretender.

Ida That's it! Twelve she was.

Petey
Pretending that I'm –

Christine
– doing well.

Ida Together. Do it together.

Christine/Petey
My need is such
I pretend too much
I'm lonely
But no one can tell.

Oh yes I'm the Young Pretender
Adrift in a world of my own.
I play the game
But to my real shame,
You've left me to dream all alone.

Too real is this feeling
Of make-believe,
Too real when I feel
What my heart can't conceal –

Petey
Oh yes I'm –

Christine Cannae believe you've got me doin this –

Valerie It's fantastic – you're wonderful!

Petey
  – *the Young* –

Christine
  – *Pretender.*

Petey/Christine
  Just laughing and gay like a clown,
  I seem to be what I'm not, you see,
  I'm wearing my heart like a crown,
  Pretending that you're still around.
  I seem to be what I'm not, you see,
  I'm wearing my heart like a crown,
  Pretending that you're still around.

  Ida and Valerie clap.

Valerie I'm honoured to have heard that.

Christine One night only. Never again. Never, ever again.

Euan What is it with Charlie?

Petey What is it wi Charlie?

Christine Drop it right now.

Euan There's a hell of a lot of mention of him goes on here.

Ida She wasnae wantin tae hear one breath o talk o Charlie earlier.

Valerie Charlie?

Euan She was telling me all about him outside.

Petey Blushes every time he's mentioned.

Christine Shut up. I do not.

Valerie Is Charlie your boyfriend?

Ida Her boyfriend –! She wishes.

Euan Charles Edward Stuart, Val.

Ida Bonnie Prince Charlie.

Euan The Young Pretender.

Valerie Oh, I didn't even realise! Oh, that's awful!

Christine King James the Third tae you lot. The title he'd have used.

Petey Pathetic Prince Charlie.

Ida His army marched right past us here, Val, right outside, on their way tae Edinburgh.

Christine On their way tae take Edinburgh. On their way tae defeat jitterin Johnny Cope at Prestonpans.

Ida Stayed the night just up the road there in Callendar House wi the Duke o Atholl.

Petey In a wee cot, the end o the Duke's bed. A wee midge, he was. Kind enough though. Let a couple o his men share the bed wi him –

Christine You won't. You know you won't.

Petey Won't what, Christine?

Christine Get me goin, Father. Willnae work.

Petey Havenae spoke o him in ages.

Christine Good reason. The argument's over an won.

Valerie Are you interested in him, Christine?

Ida Interested –! She wanted tae run away an join his army, didn't you?

Christine I should've.

Ida I wouldnae have let you go.

Christine You couldnae have stopped me.

Ida Runnin off an gettin yourself slaughtered –

Christine They didnae get slaughtered!

Petey Culloden wasnae a slaughter, Christine?

Euan What was it? A picnic?

They laugh.

Christine The odds were against him. The odds were against him from the start.

Petey The odds were wi him – all those fuckin odd-lookin Highlanders – An then there's you chargin away on your own. If you'd even looked back once, Christine, you know what you'd have seen, don't you? You know.

Valerie What? What would she have seen?

Petey No a trace o him. Wee stick figure on the horizon beltin away on his horse. He betrayed you.

Christine Regroupin. All that was left him.

Petey Betrayed, betrayed.

Christine Let down. Abandoned.

Ida The nights they were like this. They know more than anyone.

Petey That's always been your defence. The Scots, the French, the English Jacobites – all lettin you down. You no come up wi somethin better than that? You've had enough time tae think about it.

Christine You'd lose, Dad. I'm savin you face here no getting involved.

Petey C'mon. I'm enjoyin this. Just gettin started.

Warmin up.

Ida No one knows him like Christine knows him.

Euan Total failure though, wasn't he? And an alcoholic. Why the hell he's become this romantic –

Petey O God.

Christine What's that mean?

Euan What? Alcoholic?

Christine No. I mean, you sayin that. He was an alcoholic. Is that you judgin him? Sayin he was a weak man. Is that what you're sayin here?

Euan No.

Christine That's how it sounded

Valerie It did, Euan.

Euan But he did die an alcoholic. It's a fact.

Valerie Don't listen to him. He's just being awkward. He doesn't know what he's saying.

Christine You judgin him for what he was or what he's become tae you now? Is this you takin sides, Euan? You sidin with my father against me?

Petey Are you?

Ida Course he's no. Leave the boy alone. He's tired. He's wantin his bed.

Euan I'm not taking anyone's side.

Christine Well, you should. Cause where else is there? In the middle no knowin anythin really. You should take sides. Take sides an then come wi your argument. But you have tae know where you're standin first.

Ida She's only kiddin you, Euan.

Euan Alright. That's me told. You're right. I don't know enough. Didn't know it was such a sensitive area.

Christine It's no a sensitive area at all.

Petey I thought no talkin about it for so long would've blunted your arguments, Christine. But it hasnae.

Valerie But it's interesting what you said just now, Christine – what he's become to us, isn't it, that these – what would you call it? That this – received thinking – this thinking comes down to us without us ever remembering reading about them or even studying –

Euan Valerie.

Valerie What?

Euan I think you've had enough whisky.

Valerie I'm just getting started. And I was talking. I didn't interrupt you.

Petey It's interestin.

Euan I'm more interested to know when this taxi's coming. (*Pause.*) When is the taxi coming?

Valerie We haven't phoned one yet. I forgot.

Euan You haven't phoned one yet?

Ida You're stayin here.

Valerie Ida said we should just stay.

Christine Did you? (*She looks at Petey. She begins to shake her head.*)

Ida Aye. It makes sense.

Euan I'm not staying the night here.

Ida We've a downstairs room. All ready. See the head shakin there – see that.

Christine Jesus –

Euan No. No. No way. No.

Christine (*to Petey*) She tell you about this?

Ida This has nothin tae do wi you.

Christine Fine. I'll be goin then. (*She leaves.*)

Valerie Ida, if this is going to cause a problem –

Euan I think it already has, Valerie.

Ida Dinnae listen tae her. We dinnae need her permission. This is our house and we can do what we like.

Euan I'm not staying the night. No way.

Petey Is he always so grateful?

Euan I'm sorry. Thank you for the offer but we can't. There is no way we can do this.

Valerie Why can't we? Look at you. The state you're in. You can't go anywhere.

Ida We'll get onto them first thing in the mornin. Or Petey'll drive you up tae Falkirk. It's just till the mornin. There's a downstairs room an two upstairs.

Valerie Give him the downstairs.

Ida Only a single bed in each.

Petey Don't think he's in any state tae –

Valerie (*laughs*) That's fine. Isn't it?

Pause.

Euan Where's the room?

Ida C'mon, I'll show you through, Euan.

Ida goes. Euan follows.

Petey What time d'you want woken, Euan?

Euan Eh – nine. Before nine. (*to Petey*) Goodnight. (*to Valerie*) I'll see you tomorrow.

> *Euan goes out.*
> *Petey holds up the whisky bottle.*

Valerie Aye, why not?

> *He pours.*

If we ever break down again, I know where to come.

> *Petey smiles at her.*
> *Ida re-enters.*

Ida He just fell intae the bed. Closed the door an fell ontae the bed like he'd come home. Country air, what was I tellin you?

Petey A last one?

Ida Aye. But maybe no the last.

> *Short pause.*

Petey (*to Valerie*) What is it?

Valerie I know one song, I think. If I can remember the words.

Ida Aye, give us it.

Valerie I'll need a minute to try and remember the whole thing. Give me a minute. I just need a minute.

> *Lights down.*

Conservatory.

Ida's setting out a large breakfast on the table in front of the couch.

Euan's just entered.

Euan Morning.

Ida Good mornin –! How are you? How're you feelin? You feelin better?

Euan I'm feeling much better.

Ida How'd you sleep in there – mattress wasnae too hard?

Euan No. I slept great. I feel fantastic. That's the best night's sleep I've had in a long time. Must be the air, Ida, you were right.

Ida The air an the quiet, what've I been tellin you?

Euan Yeah, it is quiet. And you've cooked breakfast for me as well, Ida – you're a star, is there no end to you?

Ida Sit yourself down, then.

Euan No, I'm joking, I'm joking, I don't –

Ida Another o your jokes? I dinnae get them.

Euan I only want a cup of coffee.

Ida Will you just sit down an get on wi it? C'mon. I'm wantin tae get on.

Euan I'm not eating Petey's breakfast, Ida.

Ida D'you see anyone else in here? It's yours. An you can spare me your no, no, no, I can't, Idas. Just stand an gaze at it. That's a farmer's breakfast.

Euan Alright. I won't say a word. I'll do as I'm told. It's truly a thing of wonder, Ida.

Ida You can come back, you can. Breakfast I was always the best at – never bothered much wi lunch – it was never somethin we ate except at weekends. Dinner I was back on form – I liked makin the dinner – but breakfast – You make dinner but you cook breakfast. There's somethin about it, settin you up for the day, sendin Petey out wi it inside him. Your Valerie, she could only manage half o it.

Euan Where is she?

Ida She's been up a while.

Euan On a Sunday morning? Doesn't sound like any Valerie I know.

Ida Her an Petey left about an hour ago.

Euan Left? Did the van come? Have they gone to get my car? What time is it?

Ida He's taken her tae see the Wall.

Pause.

Euan She didn't wake me?

Ida I think she tried but you were out cold.

Euan I thought there was nothing to see.

Ida Dinnae be listenin tae Christine. There's enough tae see if you know where tae look. An Petey knows his stuff. You can go another time. Petey'll take you. Or Christine, if there's sense back in her head. Two o you arenae gettin on, even though it's none o my business, are you?

Euan Me and Christine?

Ida You an Valerie.

Euan Yeah. We are. What's Christine been tellin you?

Ida Christine's told me nothin. An, Euan, I wouldnae go confidin in her.

Euan I wasn't confiding, I was . . . we were just talking.

Ida She spotted the same thing as I did then? She's got a scaldin pair o eyes on her, Christine. She'll sniff anythin out you put in front o her.

Euan What same thing? What d'you mean? What're you talking about? There's nothing to sniff out. We're fine. I don't want to talk about it.

Ida An the two o you comin out here, was just a drive, wasn't it?

Euan Yeah.

Ida Wasnae anythin else?

Euan Whatever anythin else is – no.

Ida You'll marry her, then?

Euan I'm enjoying this, Ida. Can I get on and finish it?

Ida Gives you strength – bein married. Look at these arms. That's pushin Petey away all these years. Everyone should get married.

   Christine enters.

Christine Who's gettin married?

Ida Euan might be if he can sort out his problems wi Val.

Euan Ida – for God's sake, I don't want to talk about my private life right now!

Ida I'm sorry. I apologise.

   Pause.

Euan That's alright. (*Beat.*) This is fantastic.

Christine That's where the last o the eggs went then, is it? That's a full Scottish – makes your arteries fair burst wi pride, does it no? D'you know the difference between a full Scottish an a full English?

Euan What?

Christine With the Scottish you don't get Cumberland sausage. In memory o the slaughtered.

Euan Is that right?

Ida I have tae be gettin on. (*Ida goes out.*)

Christine I said it before, Euan, you're a topic o interest – like a weather front or a misbehavin cow – somethin tae talk about for a couple o days. She cannae help her curiosity.

Euan I didn't mean to sound – But she was talking about something –

Christine Personal. I know. But it's like you're a piece of fruit an the personal's where all the juice is so she goes straight for it, tearing your skin off tae get at it. Naw, she deserved that – interferin old – Me an my dad've had tae put up wi that for centuries. We've no personal left.

Euan You get on better wi him, don't you?

Christine Aye, always have. But she hasnae been all on her own. I had a brother.

Euan 'Had' a brother?

Christine Aye.

Euan Is he alive or dead?

Christine Dead? Are you no listenin? He's somewhere around – he's older.

Euan What's he do?

Christine Works. I'm no sure. It wasnae the life for him so he got out.

Euan And you were left holding the fort?

Christine That's one way o lookin at it.

Euan I admire that.

Christine I don't want your admiration. (*Beat.*) An I could've gone out last night if I'd wanted tae – I just didnae fancy it. The pub where I work in Greenhill, I could've gone there.

Euan I wasn't even thinking about that – it wasn't even in my head. I'm glad you didn't go – I enjoyed your singing.

Christine That was for him, no for you. Surprised you heard any o it sunk down dyin on that couch there. You were just passin through – you don't know what it's like here. You don't know a thing.

Short pause.

Euan When I woke up this morning I didn't know where I was, it was so quiet. Completely silent. And I noticed last night – the place is empty.

Christine You did have a look around you then. You did use your eyes.

Euan I thought farmers had to work all the hours God sent them – I thought they had to work dawn till dusk just to make ends meet.

Christine They do. They have tae. (*Pause.*) We're leavin. Duncan Craig, next-door neighbour's, bought us over. Those ends you're talkin about – we couldnae get them tae meet. Did all we could but just couldnae do it – losin money hand over fist. The land's no ours any more – just the house – he doesnae need the house.

Euan So you're selling up?

66

Christine Sell it tae some moneyed folk from the east or the west who're wantin a weekend retreat. Naw, that's what we're doin – retreatin. We should just burn the place down. Like the Romans did. Leave nothing behind – leave nothin anyone can use. Keep it tae yourself – it's still personal tae my mum – it's shameful. It's impossible to make a livin doin this, so why feel shame? But they do. Despite everythin, that's all they feel.

Euan Where're you going to go?

Christine (*shrugs*) See how much we get, then see. Have tae be somewhere smaller anyway. An forget a fuckin conservatory. I hate this fuckin thing anyway.

Euan You're going with them? Wherever you go you're going with them?

Short pause. She's looking at him.

Christine Aye. Why?

Ida appears in the doorway.

Ida You finished?

Euan I've left a bit. I did the best I could.

Ida I'll take it away then. She been botherin you?

Euan No.

Christine Tellin him all sorts o things – you wouldnae believe. (*She gets up.*) I'm goin for a walk. You want tae come?

Euan Yeah. Yeah, I'll come.

Ida Where're you goin?

Christine Dunno. Walkin.

Ida Well, don't go too far. Euan needs tae be back.

Euan and Christine leave by the conservatory door.

Valerie and Christine sitting in the conservatory. Pause.

Valerie Where did you go?

Christine Up the long road, over the top, then back round.

Short pause.

Valerie It's windy.

Pause.

Christine He's phonin them again – Euan. That's where he is.

Valerie Oh, right.

Christine They'll get tae you this time.

Valerie They better do. They've had enough directions to get here and back ten times.

Short pause.

Christine I'm right, am I no? No a lot there, is there? The Wall.

Valerie No – not a lot – but –

Christine Oh – a but thrown in. But what?

Valerie You get something.

Christine Do you?

Valerie Yeah. There's something about it definitely. You can imagine – y'know. You can –

Christine Imagine? Active imagination you must have. Imagine what? What were you imaginin?

Valerie Well – a sense of – what it must've been like. Your dad –

Christine And you believed it all?

Valerie He's very knowledgeable.

Christine He could embellish for Scotland, him.

Valerie I don't think he was doing that.

Christine See if you could patent a word so naebody else'd use it, that'd be mine. What would yours be? Your word?

Valerie I don't know. Patent a word? So that'd mean money, wouldn't it? – every time. So – let me think – What'm I always calling Euan?

Christine But you don't know much about them, do you? So he could've been embellishin.

Valerie He made it sound very – exciting. That's what he did.

Christine What's it like, then? Tell me. Standin on a garrison station starin across a strange, unfamiliar wilderness, God knows who's lyin in wait over the horizon. (*Pause.*) What did he tell you? We used tae swap sides just for the hell o it, choose a side o the wall tae stand on – tae get the argument goin. The Wall was a perimeter or a line o defence? What was he sayin?

Valerie That it was a perimeter.

Christine Cause who'd want north o here? All those mountains an bogs. Waste o time an manpower, eh? An who'd want tae go tae the bother o fightin them stinkin Caledonian hordes, eh? Naw, leave them tae scrap amongst themselves. Was that his line?

Valerie I think so.

Christine Make it easier for you, Val, get you involved. You're from the west so you're one o the Damnonii. Your homeland's the Clyde Valley. A tribe that never made peace wi the Romans – we were the Votadini, we did, tradin an that. But always wanted tae know why you didnae. Me an my dad always admired you for that. What was it about them? Did you no trust them? What was it?

Valerie I can't compete with you, Christine.

Christine I'm no askin you tae compete. Is that what you think I'm doin? I'm no. I'm only playin wi you.

Valerie When we were walking back he said to me –

Christine What?

Valerie This area – the land around here – your dad said it was loser's land.

Short pause.

Christine He said that?

Valerie There'd been victories, yeah, but most of it was losing, most of it was lost causes.

Christine Jesus – That's a new line o argument he's sharpenin there. See when you've got men beat, Val, they always come up wi somethin tae save themselves, do they no?

Valerie Yeah, they do. The way you speak, Christine.

Christine What? How do I speak?

Valerie You're wise beyond your years, d'you know that? Way beyond your years.

Christine Worries me for when I get older – what'll be left tae think?

Valerie Oh, there'll be plenty. Get involved with a man and you'll have plenty to think about. (*Pause.*) I think the Romans just got homesick for Rome – for the sun and the ice cream and the pavement cafés – I think that's why they left.

Christine You've been tae Rome, eh? You must've. Way you said pavement café like that. See, it's hard for me tae even say it, such a foreign concept.

Valerie I've been once.

Christine So – what's it like? C'mon.

Valerie A miracle of a city. I don't know – how it manages to – People live at a hundred miles an hour but behind them is this vast – stillness. I fell in love with it.

Christine Was this wi –?

Valerie No. I was seeing – boy before – but I went on my own actually. He couldn't go and no one else wanted to or they had no money, something like that, so I ended up going on my own.

Christine That's what I'd do. I'd go on my own. It's where Charlie Stewart died.

Valerie I know.

Christine But no because o that. I'd want tae sit an drink wine outside, at a pavement café an wear sunglasses on top o my head, find out why the hell they do that. I wouldn't want tae see or know anythin about the history – no at first. I'd sit and drink wine and order food and watch livin people.

Valerie Antipasti.

Christine Aye, but I'd want a starter first. Maybe some salami or somethin – an olives an red peppers an – You no goin tae correct me?

71

Valerie No. I know you know what antipasti is. (*Pause.*) You'll get there. You'll get to Rome, Christine.

Christine How d'you know that? How d'you know what'll happen?

Valerie I don't. But it sounds better than saying you'll never get to Rome, doesn't it? Sounds a bit better. I was trying to be enthusiatic, Christine. Sorry, maybe I overdo it sometimes.

Short pause.

Christine What did you go for? Why Rome?

Valerie I wasn't being straight with you. There was a guy involved.

Christine Was there? Who was this?

Valerie A guy called John.

Christine Oh aye. Illicit liaison, was it? An where'd you meet him?

Valerie He was standing on a balcony, waving at me and hundreds of others.

Christine Aw – Right. I see now. You're one o them. An no ashamed o it.

Valerie Who was curious about it when she was younger.

Christine Funny – I didnae have you down as one. Course my natural flamboyance gives me away.

Valerie Not that it matters whether we are or not. Whether anyone is.

Christine No. No out here. Back at your bit, aye, no out here.

Valerie But it's always there, though, isn't it? Knowing you are. In a good way. For me.

72

Christine Aye, maybe. Sometimes.

Valerie When you need help.

They look at each other and smile.
Euan enters. Conscious at first he may be
interrupting.

Christine Hello.

Valerie What did they say?

Euan 'A thousand apologies to you, sir, he's on his way
to you now.'

Valerie Good. Finally.

Euan I'm going to get some compensation from them for
this. Keeping us waiting like this. It's fucking ridiculous.

Valerie Compensation for what? We haven't spent
anything.

Beat.

Euan How was the Wall?

Valerie It was – not what it used to be.

Christine laughs. Then Valerie.

Euan Why didn't you wake me?

Valerie I tried.

Euan Not very hard.

Christine I'm goin upstairs. (*Christine leaves.*)

Valerie I looked in and said your name and you grunted
and turned over.

Euan I came in here and Ida said you'd gone out to the
Wall with Petey.

Valerie Yeah.

Euan It was me who wanted to go to the Wall in the first place –

Valerie Then it was me who wanted to come out for a drive in the first place. Euan –

Euan You could've tried a bit harder to wake me, that's all I'm saying.

Valerie Euan, I left your mobile behind on purpose. (*Pause.*) I did it on purpose.

Euan You're joking? You're joking.

Valerie I told you I wanted a day to ourselves.

Euan (*short laugh*) Val, we can still have a day to ourselves – I can still do that with my phone in my pocket.

Valerie A special day.

Euan Cause I could've just turned it off – and turned it back on in case of emergency. Why's it special? What day is it?

Valerie Yesterday was Saturday. What do you want, Euan? I need to know what you want. Two and a half years. Is something going to come of this?

Euan That's why we came out here? That's why my mobile's lying back at home on the kitchen table? This was all to be decided on one day?

Valerie Yeah.

Euan But surely the fact I'm here with you –

Valerie I knew you were going to say that!

Euan That's good enough for me. That's persuasive enough for me. Why isn't it for you?

Valerie It's not about being – near me. You don't understand. You can be near someone and still –

Euan – be a hundred miles away. I know. But I'm not a hundred miles away, am I – in those terms, am I? Putting it like that?

Valerie No. I want to know where we both think we're going. That was why I wanted yesterday.

Euan The special day –

Valerie To hear you tell me where you think we're going.

Euan I can't talk about it here. I can't talk about it now. (*Beat.*) I want to know how many miles away you think I am? Fifty – twenty-five? I'm serious – it'd help me. Where on the scale?

Valerie D'you think this is a joke? This is pointless.

Euan Was this like an ultimatum special day? Was it going to be an ultimatum, Val? Because – (*Beat.*) Jesus –

Ida's voice from just inside the house.

Ida What're you standin there for? Take them in.

Petey enters with Ida. He's carrying two cups.

He's standin in the recess there dreamin.

Petey sets down one of the cups for Euan.

Petey You didnae want one, that right, Val?

Ida (*to Valerie*) They're on their way, did Euan tell you?

Valerie No. But thanks for letting me know.

Ida 'Thanks'. You're so polite, Valerie. It's a credit tae you. Last time I heard thanks in this house was 1973.

Valerie I think I'm going to go outside for some fresh air. (*She looks at Euan.*) You coming, Euan –?

Ida Before you go, Val – the – what I gave you last night. You had a look at it?

Valerie Oh. Yeah. Yeah, I did. I'll just go up and get it. (*Valerie goes out.*)

Ida That coffee alright?

Euan What did you give her last night?

Ida Val? The accounts. Our accounts.

Petey Gave them tae her tae have a look at.

   Beat.

Euan Valerie doesn't know anything about accounts.

Ida We're just wantin her opinion. We trust her an /

Euan Ida, did you hear me? – Valerie's not an accountant.

Petey She's studied it though. That's what she was tellin us last night.

Euan Yeah, but that was years ago. That was – eight, ten years ago.

Ida It's no somethin you forget in a hurry, is it?

Petey It's somethin you cannae do for the life of you, no somethin you forget.

Ida We just want tae see what she thinks.

Euan She's not in any position to tell you what she thinks –! She's not a professional. You need professional people –

   Valerie re-enters.

Val, what're you doing? What're you doing looking at their accounts –?

Valerie I can't find them.

Euan You're not an accountant –

Valerie They're not there, Ida. Did you take them back?

Ida I havenae touched them. (*to Petey*) Did you touch them?

Petey Naw, you know how I feel about touchin them.

Valerie They asked me, Euan. It's the least I can do. I'm not an accountant but I know about accountancy.

Euan A year, what – eight, ten years ago?

Ida I'll go up and look again.

Valerie They're not there.

Christine appears in the house doorway. She's holding up a folder and some worn A4 envelopes – the accounts.

Christine This'll be what you're lookin for, is it?

Short pause.

Ida Have you been in her room?

Christine It's no her room –!

Ida You went in an took them!

Christine I want tae know what's she got them for.

Valerie Your mum asked me to look at them.

Ida Give me them. (*Ida takes the accounts from Christine.*)

Christine You hardly know these people!

Euan She's right. You hardly know us. Valerie, we hardly know them.

Christine An why's she lookin at them – why?

Petey Your mother just wanted a second opinion.

Christine It's got nothin tae do wi opinion. It's facts!

77

Valerie Christine, it won't take me long just to have a /

Euan Valerie, for God's sake!

Valerie What? What's wrong with trying to help?

Euan Because you don't know –

Valerie What?

Ida She doesn't know what?

Euan What the – situation is here.

Ida Has she been talkin tae you? Is that the word she's been usin – situation?

Valerie What is the situation?

Ida What're you doin tellin him?

Christine So I should've kept my mouth shut an handed over our accounts tae a total stranger instead?

Ida It's no the same thing!

Valerie I'm not a *total* stranger. I –

Euan Valerie, for God's sake –!

Christine We decided this already!

Ida You decided it!

Christine (*to Petey*) We agreed on this. We sat down and we agreed.

Ida So I've changed my mind. I'm allowed tae do that in my own home. I'm allowed tae do that *for* my own home!

Petey Christine, what're we goin tae do in a house in Falkirk? How're we goin tae live there? We're no cut out for livin there.

Valerie Is this to do with the accounts? What's happening?

   Beat.

Petey We sold the farm, Valerie. Sale went through a month ago.

Ida An I don't see what's wrong wi tryin tae fight back.

Christine Aw for Christ's sake! I saw this! I saw this happenin.

Ida Did you hell –!

Christine I just wanted tae see how far you were goin tae take it.

Ida You havenae been lookin at us – you've been lookin out there – a house on some Falkirk estate.

Christine One OK from her and that's fine, everythin's fine, we turn round a hundred an eighty, go back on everythin.

Valerie What're you going back on? What're you talking about?

Ida We can make it work! I can make it work! Petey an me can make it work.

Christine Bed an breakfast! Bed an fuckin breakfast! D'you hear that? Bed an fuckin breakfast –

Ida Dinnae laugh at it! Dinnae laugh! You've laughed enough!

Petey Ida –

Christine I cannae stop bloody laughin! Bed an fuckin breakfast.

Ida Petey, stop her. Valerie –

Petey Christine –

Christine You been taken in again, Dad?

Valerie Why not? It's not impossible is it?

Euan Valerie, will you keep out /

Ida There you are – see!

Christine Bed an breakfast. Out here? For the hordes o visitors that flock here like you? You dinnae know the first thing you're talkin about.

Ida Dinnae talk tae her like that.

Christine Bed an fuckin breakfast.

Ida You laugh one more time an I'll throw this (*cup of tea*) in your face, Christine.

Petey Ida –

Christine I'd like tae see you try.

Ida I would, God help me.

Petey Ida!

Ida It's her! Get her out o here. I dinnae want tae look at you.

Euan (*getting to his feet*) We'd better go outside.

Christine I'm feelin this as much as you.

Ida Are you? Doesnae seem like it.

Christine It was the best for us, Dad. We sat in here an decided that. As a family.

Ida What family were you sittin wi? No this one!

Christine It's all we can do!

Ida Dinnae say 'we'! There's you an there's us.

Christine looks at them, then walks out. Silence.

She willnae even give the idea a chance.

Euan Valerie. Let's go outside.

Ida You dinnae have tae.

Euan We're going to wait for the van on the road.
Valerie – we'll wait for the van on the road. Outside.
I'm sorry about all this. Valerie, are you coming?

Ida Wait –

Petey Let them go, Ida.

Valerie Sorry about this? Is that me? Are you apologising
for me? You saying this is my fault?

Euan No, I was /

Valerie What? What were you saying?

Petey I'll just go and see if she's – (*Petey goes out.*)

Valerie Mm? Because I was trying to be helpful. I was
trying to help them.

Ida That's all she was doin – helpin. An it's appreciated.

Valerie D'you know what that is, Euan, do you –?

Euan I'm going outside. (*to Ida*) Thanks for putting us
up /

Valerie Walking away again – Why don't you run!

Euan leaves by conservatory door. Short pause.

Ida It's no your fault at all, Val. We asked you.

Valerie No, but it is my fault. Because I was concerned
about you – so it is my fault. I will not allow people –
anyone – not even him – he's the last person I want
feeling embarrassed because of me because – because
I was trying to help someone out!

Ida You go ahead and say it. If it's there, it's better said.
Only need tae look at us, tae understand that.

Valerie Jesus Christ!

Ida You did help. You read them (*the accounts*). You
listened tae me.

Valerie I'm still not going to say it'll work but it's a brave thing to do, Ida, it's a brave thing to be thinking of. I admire you for it – I do.

Ida I know.

Petey enters.

Petey She wouldnae come out her room.

Ida Och, leave her in there, then. We can do it, Petey. She said we could.

Valerie Ida, I /

Ida But what I'm sayin is it's no impossible. It's better than fossilisin isn't it, on some estate in Falkirk. Isn't it, Val? Better than fossilisin an then dyin, trapped somewhere like that where we dinnae know a soul.

Valerie Of course it is. To lose this house after all these years –

Petey (*to Valerie*) Were you goin, aye?

Ida What're you sayin tae her?

Petey Dinnae mean to be rude but – This's somethin between us, Ida.

Valerie No. You're right, Petey, I'll go.

Ida You stay right there if you want.

Petey Ida, let the girl go.

Euan opens the conservatory door.

Euan The van's here, if you're interested.

A look between him and Valerie.
An orange light shines into the conservatory from the truck.

Valerie I'll phone you. I've got your number.

Ida Aye, do that. An come back, Val. You can be the first couple tae stay here.

Christine appears in the house doorway. She's holding a coat and a small bag she's packed.

Christine Can I get a lift wi you, Euan?

Pause.

Petey Where're you goin, Christine?

Christine Leavin – what's it look like? (*to Euan*) Can I? There's room in the car, isn't there?

Petey Christine, you cannae.

Christine You dinnae need me. You're makin decisions on your own now. I'm no needed.

Petey Course you are.

Christine (*to Euan*) Can I? Think you owe me this, d'you no?

Valerie (*to Euan*) Owe her?

Christine Aye – we helped you out, Val, did we no? Now you can help me out. Help me get out o here.

Petey Christine, dinnae go.

Valerie Have you really thought about this, Christine?

Christine You my mother now, Valerie?

Ida I wouldnae be askin that, I don't think.

Christine Naw, I'm doin it completely off the top o my head but tell you what, feels great.

Petey Ida, say somethin –

Ida She's made her mind up – what'm I goin tae say?

Christine Euan – are we goin?

Euan OK.

Christine Good. (*She walks through them to the conservatory door.*)

Petey Christine.

Christine Naw, Dad –

>   *Christine walks past Euan and out.*
>   *Euan looks at Valerie.*

Valerie You're going to take her away from her family?

Euan It's not my decision. It's hers. You coming?

Valerie I'm not getting in that car with you and her.

Ida I wouldnae. No wi her burnin like that –

Euan You're not coming?

Valerie No. And you're going, are you?

>   *Pause.*

Euan Yeah.

Valerie Bye then.

>   *Pause. He leaves.*

Country road.
   Christine's looking at Euan's map. Euan's looking at her.

Christine What was it then? What's the diagnosis?

Euan Clutch cable. Your dad was right.

Christine Hope he apologised for bein almost twenty-four hours late, did he?

Euan Twenty-four hours late and a ten-minute job.

Christine We're on the fold – did you know? Right on the fold.

Euan Yeah, I saw that.

Christine Nae wonder you didnae know where you were. (*Beat.*) We're still goin, aren't we? You're no havin second thoughts?

Euan Don't say it like that –! Sounds like we're eloping or something.

Christine Elopin –! Hadnae thought o that. (*Beat.*) You are. Second thoughts. I can see it.

Euan It's not about having second thoughts.

Christine Fuck, I knew I should've hitched with that mechanic man.

Euan It's about thinking this through.

   Short pause.

Christine Right. That's me done. Thought it through. Answer's still the same. No think I havenae lain in my bed thinkin this through for years?

Euan I don't know – have you? I thought you were in love with this place. I thought you could never leave.

Christine It's me that's ready tae go here! It's you I'm waitin on so I can leave! You cannae let me down now. Are we goin?

Euan Will you just give me one minute here! It's not you I'm really thinking about right at the moment, Christine.

Christine Fair enough. (*Pause.*) Will she be wantin you tae go back for her, d'you think?

Euan I don't know.

Christine Cause I'd just want a clean cut, clean split, y'know? Nae mess. Nae entrails.

Euan gives her a look. Short pause.

Euan I don't know what she'll be wanting.

Christine Her own office. If she's serious about settin up as a fuckin small business advisor.

A short laugh from Euan.

Laughin's good. It's a start.

Euan What do I do here? What do I do what do I do?

Christine She was way way out o order lookin at those accounts. They're private accounts. Fuckin shockin pathetic embarrassin accounts but still private accounts.

Euan Your mother asked her to look at them.

Christine All she needed tae say was no.

Euan She's not like that. She wouldn't have said no.

Christine Stickin up for her now? We're no goin tae get the great reunion now, are we? Runnin towards each other, arms out, across a non-profit-yieldin field.

Euan We've been together almost three years.

Christine We were in the black three years ago, then it was red, red, all systems red.

Euan And today could be the end of that.

Christine Will be for me when I hear that engine revvin. (*Pause.*) West coast thing, is it? Agonisin?

Euan For fuck's sake, it's three years of my life!

Pause. Christine's about to speak but Euan holds his hand up for silence. Long pause.
Euan smirks briefly to himself.

Christine What?

Euan Thought if she doesn't come back – but she has to come back, she has to get her stuff, she's got all her stuff at my place – but if she leaves, if she moves out then – life with her not there. Life without her. Shouldn't even be thinking this but the thought's there and the sky hasn't fallen in and it's almost – it's almost – a thrill to think it. Thrilling. Could I do that? I don't think I could. It would be so easy to do if I wanted to. Val would be gone. (*He begins to move around, as if to shake himself out of this.*)

Christine She'll come home tomorrow, I bet you, tail between her legs, ears chewed off by the two o them.

Pause.

Euan They're going to miss you.

Christine Naw, they'll have tae learn tae do without me – that's different. We'd decided what we were doin – if they want tae stay on an humiliate themselves, let them. I'm

87

gettin away an nothin's stoppin me. I'm so excited – I'm feelin twenty again.

Euan You are twenty.

Christine An it's a great age tae be. Whole world in front o you. An goin west tae find out what all the fuss is about.

Euan What're you going to do?

Christine When?

Euan When we get there.

Christine I'll find somethin.

Euan Who're you going to stay with?

Christine I'll find someone. I know people.

Euan You can't stay with me, Christine.

Christine Thanks.

Euan I never said –

Christine I never asked. Did you hear me ask? I know other people. (*Indicates back in direction of farm.*) They're no everythin I've got. I've got my brother, I can phone him. (*Beat.*) You'll show me some things though, won't you? Where tae go an that. How tae find a place.

Euan If you're twenty again you won't want to go to the same places I do.

Christine But I can come round a couple o times – tae see your place.

Euan Yeah.

Christine Aye right. Dinnae believe you for a second.

Euan You can.

Christine You don't want tae see me again once I get out o that car. It's OK, I understand. (*Beat.*) Can I stay tonight? Just tonight? I havenae got anywhere for tonight.

   Pause.

Euan Yeah. You can stay tonight, but only tonight.

Christine Wouldnae want tae stay at yours more than one night anyway.

Euan Good. Cause that's all you are staying.

Christine Wouldnae want tae sleep on some smelly old sofa –

Euan We've a spare bed. And our sofa doesn't smell.

Christine A spare bed – that'll do.

   Pause.

Euan It's not going to happen, Christine.

Christine What's not goin tae happen?

Euan What you're thinking.

Christine What'm I thinkin?

   Short pause.

Euan Doesn't matter.

Christine No, say it. Somethin's obviously on your mind.

Euan Forget it.

   Pause.

Christine Fuck, is that what you were thinkin –? You were way ahead o me there. Is that what you were wantin tae do tae me, man your age?

Euan Drop it. Shut up.

Pause.

Christine When did you see me that way?

Euan Christine –

Christine First. Was it when I first came in? Or was it later? Did you come round tae thinkin o me like that or was it when you first saw me? I want tae know.

Euan When I saw you I didn't flirt with you.

Christine I know. Hard tae flirt when you're nickin a book from me. An later –? Did I do anythin that made you –

Euan Were you trying to do anything?

Christine I might've been. So when was it?

Pause.

Euan It might've been since we've been waiting here.

Pause.

Christine But what'm I doin?

Euan (*looking off*) Shit.

Christine looks in that direction.

Christine Aw, Jesus, no –

After a moment, Petey enters. He's out of breath.

Petey Got you.

Christine What're you doin? What're you runnin for?

Petey I was goin tae jump in the car but couldnae find the keys – you got them? You used it last.

Christine goes into her pocket, brings out the keys.
Petey still hasn't looked at Euan and won't until Euan addresses him.

Christine Aye, they're here. (*She hands them to him. Short pause.*) It was the clutch cable – you were right.

Petey Aye. (*Beat.*) Am I goin tae be able tae talk you out o this?

Christine No, I dinnae think so.

Short pause.

Petey What would we do if we're no here, Christine? It was when I started thinkin about that. What would we do?

Christine It's nothin tae do wi me now.

Petey Dinnae say that.

Christine I'm already thinkin about other things. I'm thinkin about myself – that no what she told me tae do?

Petey She didnae mean it like that.

Christine You always used tae say that, Dad. She didnae mean it like that. She didnae mean it. But she did. She does. She always means everythin. For good or bad, she always means everythin. (*Beat.*) We've come tae the end. Can you no see that? This is the end. I'm goin tae get intae the car now. (*Christine begins to walk off in direction of Euan's car.*)

Petey So you're just walkin out on us? Washin your hands. Off tae the west, God knows where.

Euan Mr Cauldwell, I –

Petey I dinnae want tae hear from you, son. I dinnae want tae talk to you. I dinnae want you in my sight.

Euan Why? What've I done?

Petey You've been fillin my daughter's head.

Euan No I haven't –!

91

Christine Maybe it's been needin tae be filled.

Euan I haven't said a thing to her. I think she's smart enough to –

Christine Euan, c'mon.

Petey They dinnae understand us, Christine – remember that.

Euan We don't understand what? Who's 'we'?

Petey They don't understand how we are. What we've done.

Euan What've you done? What're you talking about? What've you done?

Petey How hard we've worked all these years.

Euan I work hard. Most of the people I know work hard.

Petey What's it you do, then? What line you in?

Euan Doesn't matter what I do.

Petey You've seen the insides o us, let's hear yours.

Euan I work fuckin hard – that's all you need to know.

Petey You've been wantin rid o us. The lot o you.

Euan Aw, right – yeah. The lot of us. Course we did. Nothing else on our minds.

Petey Started wi the miners.

Euan (*laughs*) The miners? Did it? What did they do?

Petey That strike back in the eighties.

Euan Uh-huh. Yeah. I remember it.

Petey Government dragged it out, stood up tae them. Resultin in what? Energy shortage. Exactly what they wanted. Killed off two birds wi one stone.

Euan First bird being the miners, right? And the second bird – who? You?

Petey Aye. Cause an energy shortage meant that cattle-feed factories werenae able tae heat their furnaces hot enough so's tae kill off all the bacteria. Listen – dinnae laugh. It's known. Healthy cattle were fed wi animal remains full o bacteria. That was the start o the BSE. Cows fallin in the fields. Beef banned. Nobody trustin us – naebody buyin from us. That's how we're bein gotten rid o.

Euan That is bullshit, Petey. Where the hell did you get that from?

Petey You're livin in another country, son.

Euan You should visit us sometime.

Euan walks off towards the car. Pause. Petey follows him.

Petey See if anythin happens tae her –

3.2

Ida and Valerie in the conservatory.

Valerie Fifteen.

Ida Fifteen?

Valerie Fifteen definitely.

Ida No twenty?

Valerie I really think fifteen, Ida.

Ida Fifteen?

Valerie Fifteen's reasonable. You have to think about what you're offering.

Ida I'm thinkin about what we're offerin –! A peaceful quiet secluded room for the night and one o my farmer's breakfasts in the mornin – twenty pound too much for that?

Valerie Fifteen's more realistic, I think.

Ida Do you?

Valerie You might even want to think about an introductory offer.

Ida A what?

Valerie A low price to get people out here.

Ida I know what it is. We have tae make this worth our while, Val.

Valerie Alright. If you want twenty, we'll say twenty.

Ida There's no point if we dinnae. There's no one else out here doin this, Val, remember that. That's a strength. We're a monopoly. (*Beat.*) Maybe fifteen is more realistic –

Valerie Tell you what, Ida, I'll work it out for both of them, OK? Fifteen and twenty. See how they compare. Alright?

Ida Much were you thinkin o for this introduction offer?

Valerie I don't know. Ten.

Ida Ten! No. Ten –! What kind o figure's that?

Valerie You need to get people out here, Ida, that's the bottom line.

Ida That's scrapin the bottom line – ten! We're no runnin a poorhouse. We'd advertise an everythin. Get the word out. Newspapers, magazines an that.

Valerie So you'll have to put money aside for advertising –

Ida An how much is that goin tae be?

Valerie However much it's going to be. I can't give you an exact figure.

Ida But once the word gets round.

Valerie Yeah – once. But the word getting round, Ida –

Ida I know how word gets round.

Valerie But that word has to start somewhere, d'you see? That word has to be spread by people who've seen the ad and come here and had a good time and think it's a good deal and start telling their friends that they really have to come, they don't know what they're missing, it's a unique experience.

Ida But that could be you. You could start the word when you get back, couldn't you? You could start spreadin it.

Valerie Yeah, but d'you see what I've been saying? It's all connected. How much you put in affects how much you get back. You can't just rely /

Ida I know that –! How much I put in –! I know. D'you no think I don't know that livin here all these years?

Valerie Of course you do. I didn't mean to – Sorry if it sounded like that.

Ida Gets me jumpy this money talk. Always has. I don't need you addin tae it – I need you tae be calm and sensible an give me a figure for all o this.

Valerie OK. Calm and sensible.

Ida It's futures on that piece o paper there.

Valerie I know it is.

Ida An you're goin tae need another column on the side there for the extras.

Valerie Extras? What extras? What're the extras?

Ida Petey takin them tae the Wall like he took you – that's the extras. We could charge for that – no? You'd have paid for that, wouldn't you? Learnin all that knowledge.

Valerie OK. I'll draw another column on the side. There. Another column.

Ida But Petey'd make it intae a proper tour. There's enough there, isn't here?

Valerie Yeah. Yeah, I think so. It'd have to go to the other sites as well of course, what's it called?

Ida Aye, there's three or four sites – that's enough. Why could those Romans no have built it wi stone, eh? We'd be rivallin Hadrian's – folk'd be flockin. Could they no have thought o us when they were buildin it? (*Beat.*) Another extra – Petey could take them round the farm – show them how we lived, couldn't he? If they bring kids the kids'll love that, won't they?

Valerie D'you think Duncan would agree to that?

Ida Course he would. I'd ask Susannah. They'd let us. We wouldnae be touchin anythin.

Valerie You should ask Petey, see what he thinks.

Ida But it's what we did. We know better than anyone. (*Shouts.*) Petey –! Where is he? Petey –! He always answers me first time.

Valerie (*getting up*) My head's swimming with all these figures.

Ida's gone to the door into the house.

Ida Petey!

Valerie Ida –!

Ida What?

Valerie My head's killing me. Can you keep it down a bit?

Ida Is it? Sorry. He always answers me. He must've gone out. I'm sorry, Val.

Valerie No, it's – it's nothing.

Ida Euan said he'd had the best night's sleep he'd had in years. You'd come again, Val, eh? You'd tell people?

Valerie Of course I'd come, Ida. Of course I would. With or without him.

Ida Better with him cause we could charge you double then.

Valerie Does he really always answer you first time?

Ida Petey? Naw. Sometimes. But he's never too far away.

Short pause.

Valerie D'you know, Ida – Euan. That f – bastard, bastard of a boyfriend. D'you know what he does? D'you know what he doesn't do? Sometimes – when he's in the flat and I call him like you just did, I call out his name – he doesn't answer. He doesn't answer.

Ida Maybe he hasnae heard.

Valerie It's a one-bedroom flat, Ida.

Ida What's wrong wi him, then?

Valerie And it's not that he's ignoring me, it's cause he's in his own world, he's so much in his own head half the time that I don't even register – I'm on the outside calling in. Right, that's enough about that. I don't want to talk about this. We have to do this. We have to finish this. How many rooms?

Ida You sure?

Valerie I'll do figures for both – fifteen and twenty. How many rooms? One downstairs –

Ida No, I was thinkin Petey and me'd move downstairs – makes it four upstairs. Four wi Christine's. We'd have tae gut it first an send her stuff on but it's four.

Valerie She might want to come back, Ida.

Ida Christine? What's more important? We have tae survive. If it means sacrificin her – She should know by now what kind o people we are. We fight wi all we've got. It's best she's gone, it's best. She should've been out here long before now – but it was Petey. Petey held ontae her. She's her father's daughter. Could you see us leavin here? How would we? In daylight? No – the dead o night. We wouldnae be able tae look at each other, me an Petey. Our daughter, brought up here, leadin us away? No. (*Beat.*) Know what it is wi her? Know what it is wi Christine? She came too late. We had her too late.

Valerie No. You shouldn't say 'too late'. How can it ever be too late to bring a child into the world? There's no best time. There's no such thing as 'too late'.

Ida Naw, there is.

Valerie There's not.

Ida I think there is. (*Beat.*) Yours'll be late, Val. The baby you're wantin tae have.

Valerie O Jesus, is it that obvious? It can't be. Is it?

Short pause.

Ida An is he the one? Euan.

Valerie If he's not, I'm going to stop looking. I think so.

Ida You're impatient. You're wantin tae get things goin now.

Valerie Not one day goes by when I don't think – he'd be two, she'd be two or three or four. I can't stop thinking that.

Ida What's wrong wi that?

Valerie I know. I know because it'd make my life – it'd make our life – but firstly it'd make my life so much – so much – fuller. And more rewarding. So much richer. Instead of this – this – this – airless existence I live. This – I'm bored of everything I do – we do – because it's not what I should be doing any more. Having dinner with some friends like we were supposed to have last night – I shouldn't be there! I don't want to be there! I should be at home with the baby, the two-year-old, three-year-old baby. I should have him or her on my arm, behind me in the car, beside me in a cot in the bedroom – this is what I think every day – and if he doesn't want that – if he's stupid enough not to want that with me then he can – maybe it's the end. Cause I'm not going to let him deny me this! I'm not going to cry, I'm not going to, I'm not going to. When I go back there tonight, I still want this bottled up, I want this kept inside for when I see him tonight. Can I go to the toilet, wash my face? Then I'll come back and we'll finish this. It's going to work, Ida. I know it is.

Ida You have tae watch them when they're older though, that's the only thing.

Valerie I can see that.

Ida That they dinnae get the upper hand.

Valerie No. (*Beat.*) I'd want us to be friends, I think. Like me and my mum – it's like having a friend.

Ida It's not goin tae be as easy as you think.

Valerie I don't think it's going to be easy. I didn't say that. (*Beat.*) But you've been under so much pressure, Ida. It's bound to affect how you are with each other, isn't it?

Ida Aye.

Valerie She'll phone though, won't she? Won't she?

Ida Aye. She better. (*Beat.*) Was that you bein critical, Val?

Valerie Of what?

Ida Me an Christine. Were you bein critical o us?

Valerie No.

Ida You want tae be friends with your child? It sounded like you were criticisin an I don't think you should be.

Valerie I wasn't. I wasn't. I didn't mean it like that.

Ida Sounded like it.

Valerie I wasn't.

Pause.

Ida Go an wash your face. Naw, have a shower.

Valerie No, it's alright. Ida, I –

Ida Take a shower.

Valerie Alright. Feel like I've been in these clothes for months. Thanks.

Valerie goes out.
   Ida sits on her own for a few moments.
   From outside, the sound of car wheels. The car stops.
   Ida stands up, looks out the window, sits back down.
   After a few moments she hears someone inside the house.

Ida Petey, is that you back?

Euan enters.

Aw, it's you.

Euan Yeah.

Ida What're you doin here? I thought you'd gone.

Euan Well, I've come back.

Ida I see that. Where's Petey?

Euan I brought him back.

Ida He went after you?

Euan Yeah. Where's Valerie?

Ida An Christine? Where's she? She with him?

Euan She's sitting in the car. She didn't want me to come back but I did. She's not too pleased.

Ida No, cause she thought she was leavin. She doesnae like bein promised somethin an then no gettin it.

Euan Go out to her, Ida. Bring her back in.

Ida I'm no goin anywhere.

Euan Ida, go outside and talk to her. Go an help Petey.

Ida What'll I say?

Euan How do I know? She's your daughter. You've had twenty years to think what to say to her. Where's Valerie?

Ida She's upstairs havin a wash. (*Ida's on her feet looking through the conservatory window.*) Can she no even get out the car?

Euan Just go out to her – for God's sake.

Ida Alright. Give me my fags.

Valerie appears in the house doorway.

Valerie What's going on?

Euan I brought her back.

Ida She'll lock the door and have me standin outside there lookin like a fool.

Euan Just go.

Ida leaves.
Silence.

Valerie I thought you'd gone.

Euan No.

Valerie You saw sense, then?

Euan Yeah. I saw sense.

Valerie I can't believe you were even thinking of taking her with you.

Euan Well, I didn't. She's back with her family. What're we going to do now?

Valerie I was going to have a shower.

Euan You're going to have a shower?

Valerie Yeah.

Euan laughs. Outside, the sound of a car engine starting.

It's where I do all my best thinking, Euan, you know that. Where I make my decisions about the things that affect me day-to-day. You're not even listening –!

Euan That's my car –

He looks out the window. The car's driving off.

Valerie Is it?

Euan What the fuck's she doing?

Valerie What is it?

He's staring out of the window, taken aback. Valerie's beside him, looking out.

Euan They've taken my car –

Valerie Who? Christine?

Euan All of them! They were all inside. They've just driven off.

Valerie All of them?

Euan Yes –!

Valerie What've they done that for?

Euan I don't fucking believe this –! They've stolen my car.

Valerie Where will they go?

Euan How do I know? They've nicked my bloody car!

Valerie What happened? Did anything happen when you were –?

Euan No –! For God's sake! (*Beat.*) Petey turned up and had a go at me cause I don't understand their problems – that's all that happened. Nothing that justifies this. Nothing. Fucking hell –

Valerie What're we going to do?

Euan Phone the police?

Valerie You think we should? What will we tell them?

Euan (*a short laugh*) What will we tell them? A family of three have nicked our car. A farmer, his wife and his daughter.

Valerie She was trying to get away from them – why's she taking her parents with her? Where will they go? What direction will they go in? I can't believe Ida'd do this. I can't believe Petey would.

Euan Maybe this is another of Ida's money-spinning ideas. Fucking sightseeing tours of the district.

They both laugh.

Valerie Cauldwell Cabs.

They laugh again, longer and harder.

Euan Cauldwell Removals. (*fits of laughter*) Cauldwell – No, can't think of anything. The fucking Cauldwells!

Their laughter dies away. They look at each other. Nothing's said. Pause.

If I phone a taxi – you'll come back with me?

Valerie Yeah. We can phone the police from there.

Euan Yeah. I want to get back to the flat.

Valerie Yeah.

Euan And what happens then?

Valerie You mean –?

Euan Yeah.

Valerie I just want to get back there. I just want to get there first. I just want to be there.

Euan (*standing up*) Back to the phone.

Valerie Car –!

Euan Is it? (*Listens.*) Yeah.

Valerie Jesus –!

Euan Thank fuck for that!

They leave by the conservatory door and enter into the yard.

They stop, watch as Ida, Petey and Christine approach them.

Ida You should go now.

Euan (*to Christine*) Where's my keys? Give me the keys.

Christine In the ignition.

Ida Better you go now, Euan, Valerie, better you leave us now.

Euan What the hell were you thinking of? That's my car.

Christine I wanted a go in it. Feel it for myself. I wanted tae take my parents out for a spin.

Valerie Christine, you could've crashed it – anything could've happened.

Petey We didnae crash. She's a good driver.

Christine We didnae go very far – we stopped up the road there an had a talk tae ourselves.

Euan Good. I'm glad.

Valerie We're going to go back to our flat.

Euan We're not taking you, Christine.

Christine Aye, I know that. I can see that. I dinnae want tae come.

Euan You got everything, Val?

Valerie Yeah. Thank you, Ida.

Ida looks at her, says nothing.

Christine (*to Euan*) Were you laughin at my dad?

Euan Me?

Petey You're the only one she's lookin at.

Euan Laughing? No.

Christine I saw you. On the top road there. I was in the car. You were laughin at him.

Petey What was so funny? What was the joke?

Christine What d'you find so funny about us?

Euan You don't believe that, do you? All that stuff he was telling me?

Valerie Euan, we should get going, I think.

Christine Aye. How? D'you know different?

Euan I know that was a load of /

Valerie Euan! Can we go?

Petey You know better, do you? You didnae answer.

Euan You live out here, believing that? D'you not read anything? D'you not talk to /

Petey There's things you don't know about. There's things you can't know about.

Valerie I'm getting in the car, Euan.

Christine I'd listen tae her for once, Euan. The two o you should fuck off, I think, don't you? Nae offence.

Ida Christine –

Christine Naw, they should – both o them fuck off. But especially you, Euan, while you can.

Euan While I can?

Petey You've nothin else under your jacket, have you?

Short pause.

Euan I'd get away from here as soon as I could, Christine.

Christine What're you sayin?

Valerie Euan –!

Christine Did I hear you right?

Euan Get away from here.

Valerie Euan –

Christine You're sayin that after freeloadin off us?

Valerie Will you please get in the car now.

She walks off. Euan begins to follow.

Petey Aye, freeloaders!

Euan As fast as you can, Christine.

Christine Freeloader! Thief! You're due us! Where's our money?

Euan Money?

Petey Aye, where is it?

Euan We don't owe you anything.

Christine One night's bed an breakfast?

Euan No.

Christine One night's bed an breakfast.

Euan It was hospitality last night, I seem to remember.

Petey You owe us for one night's bed an breakfast.

Euan I'm getting out of here. (*Euan begins to walk off.*)

Christine You owe us for one night's bed an breakfast!

Petey One night's bed an breakfast!

They're walking towards the car.

Christine Oi, freeloaders! One night's bed an breakfast!

Petey One night's bed an breakfast!

The car's engine starts.

Christine One night's bed an fuckin breakfast!

Petey One night's bed an breakfast!

Christine One night's bed an fuckin breakfast!

Petey Freeloaders! Thieves! One night's bed an breakfast!

The car drives off.

Christine One night's bed an fuckin breakfast!

The car's gone.
    Silence.
    Christine and Petey turn and look at Ida. She looks at them.
    They walk from the yard into the conservatory.
    Christine and Petey sit down. Ida remains standing.

Ida They didnae even finish their breakfast. Either o them. I had tae scrape half o it away. Anyone wantin anythin?

Christine No.

Petey No. No the now.

Ida A'right. (*She moves to the door.*)

Petey Ida, come'n sit down. You've been on your feet since dawn.

Ida sits down.
    The book remains on the table between them.
    End.